Retire to the Life You Love

Practical Tools for Designing Your Meaningful Future

Nell Smith
Dec 2014

Nell Smith

Praise for Retire to the Life You Love – Practical Tools for Designing Your Meaningful Future

"Nell thoughtfully weaves inspiring stories with practical tools and resources to help answer challenging questions and engage with energy and eagerness in life design. *Retire to the Life You Love* provides a holistic view of, and comprehensive approach to, re-framing retirement from an outdated model to an energizing and *designed* phase of life. This interactive and applied book is certain to capture audiences, change mindsets, and inspire growth. Writing their story and reflecting on new thoughts and ideas along the way, readers complete a journey from self-discovery and reflection to goal-setting and action.

Sharing her story, Nell helps readers to feel understood and not alone in this tremendous life transition often plagued with uncertainty, irrelevance and isolation. This is a book not only full of wonderful insights and genuine care, but also filled with opportunities for self-reflection, awareness and discovery, filling the reader with new insights and applicable next steps. A comprehensive approach to re-thinking retirement!"

Rich Feller, Past President, National Career Development Association, and thought leader with AARP's Life Reimagined program
www.lifereimagined.aarp.org

"This book is a work of wisdom, combining practical tools, strategies and ideas into an invaluable resource. Presenting a journey through self-exploration, much of this book focuses on designing one's life in a meaningful, fulfilling way. By focusing beyond one's working career, this book beautifully pulls together the inseparable spheres of life, including relationships, health, contributing, learning and leisure. If people spent 10% of the time they spend planning their finances on planning a meaningful future, our society's happiness index would increase exponentially – this book is a way to begin this process."

Dr. Laura Hambley, Founder of Canada Career Counselling and Adjunct Professor of Psychology, University of Calgary
www.calgarycareercounselling.com

"Retire to the Life You Love reads like a conversation with a life coach. Nell deftly guides you with examples, stories, and practical tools to show you the opportunities a long life can bring for inner peace, enriched relationships, and evolving wisdom to contribute to the greater good of society."

Ken Dychtwald, Ph.D., Author, *A New Purpose: Redefining Money, Family, Work, Retirement, and Success.* www.agewave.com

"I couldn't put this jewel of a book down! In a calm and impactful way, Nell inspires you with her own story, those of her many workshop participants and those in later life. Step by practical step, she guides you to embrace your next chapter moving FROM your current career TO living every facet of your life to the fullest, your way."

Kate Jones, M.Ed, Co-author of *Retirement Dimensions*™ and *Great Parenting Skills for Navigating Your Kid's Personality*, www.skills4people.com

"What a wonderful toolkit for folks contemplating retirement as well as those who are already retired, but craving a richer experience. Grounded in the Six Circles of Life model, *Retire to the Life You Love* offers a comprehensive integrated approach to life planning that acknowledges the interconnections between all of our life roles and activities. Written by a credible and compassionate author who walks her talk, this readable, engaging, and inspiring book shares compelling case examples and offers holistic tips and strategies for customizing a satisfying and purpose-filled retirement lifestyle. You'll want to keep this book on your bookshelf, returning to it again and again to fine-tune retirement plans as new challenges and opportunities come your way."

Dr. Roberta Neault, President, Life Strategies Ltd. www.lifestrategies.ca

"As we live longer and healthier lives, more and more people are faced with the challenge and the opportunity of shaping what it is they want to do in later life. This book is timely, practical and full of self-guided activities to help you build the life you want in retirement."

Lynne Bezanson and Sareena Hopkins
Co-Executive Directors, Canadian Career Development Foundation
www.ccdf.ca

"Arriving as I am, about to retire from all professional activities in the career development field, this lively and engaging book was particularly timely for me. It raises the questions which have been in my mind, and others besides, and provides a rich resource for exploring them carefully, systematically, and creatively. It will be of great value to anyone involved in later-life career transitions, helping them to design the next stage of their lives."

Professor Tony Watts, International Policy Consultant, UK

"Using Nell's tools and resources, I am confident in the design of my retirement plan because it is based on what I love to do and who I am"

Suzen Sam, Founder, Enriched by Code
www.hiddenground.wordpress.com

"Reading Nell's book has re-energized me! After being retired for 10 years, I wanted to revisit my retirement choices. I am already using the tools and strategies to design the next new chapter of my life."

RD McLean, Retired City Auditor, City of Calgary

"When planning for retirement all too often the central focus revolves around how much money an individual has accumulated or is currently saving, whether he or she has the correct asset mix to maximize investment returns, and running projections to illustrate the type of income stream the individual can expect to receive during retirement.

Notwithstanding the importance of these issues, planning for retirement is far more than a number crunching exercise. Beyond dollars and cents, the *qualitative* aspects of retirement require more than a passing mention when constructing a comprehensive and holistic retirement plan.

In *Retire to the Life You Love*, Nell Smith puts the *quality* of your retirement front and centre. The spotlight is not on 'how much' I will have in retirement but rather, 'how well'– emotionally and physically – I will be **living** my retirement. *Retire to the Life You Love* invites the reader to look inward and examine what is truly important to the individual and how he or she would like to spend the next phase of their life.

The book contains hands-on, intuitive exercises and analytical tools to help the reader arrive at answers to the truly important questions: 'What are you going to do when you retire?' 'Who am I when I am no longer identified by my work role?' 'How do I find joy and passion in my life?' and 'What will give my life new meaning and purpose?'

Combining the lifestyle concepts raised in *Retire to the Life You Love* with traditional quantitative retirement planning is a must for anyone who is truly looking for a robust, all-encompassing and fulfilling roadmap for their golden years."

Canadian Institute of Financial Planning, www.cifp.ca

"I love Nell's work, she is a pioneer in helping KAA-Boomers design the retirement of their dreams. A must read."

Barbara Jaworski, CEO Workplace Institute
www.workplaceinstitute.org

"*Retire to the Life You Love* is one of the most insightful and practical books I have encountered to help address the next chapter of one's life. Many retirees had jobs with golden handcuffs that paid well or went down career paths according to what was available at the time, but were never really satisfying. How wonderful to have practical tools to help design the later stages of life. I will recommend it to my husband, my clients, and my friends."

Linda Berens, Author, *Understanding Yourself and Others, An Introduction to the 4 Temperaments* www.lindaberens.com

For Tom, Kathryn, Colleen, Dave, Meagan, Ryan, Matthew, Nadine, Logan, Jasper, and Kiara

ACKNOWLEDGEMENTS

Each person who I've ever talked with recently or in the past, each person who participated in the career planning, work search, and retirement workshops I facilitated, each family member, colleague, associate, friend, and acquaintance have all contributed immensely to my own understanding, respect, and appreciation of people and their individual worth. To each of you, I'm extremely grateful for being the person you are. You have informed my beliefs and the ideas in this book. Some of you have allowed me to share your stories and examples.

Specifically in the writing of this book, my friends Diana Mitchell and Karen Hinton have helped to shape my thinking towards the more spiritual realm – from doing to being. Growing out of the meaningful discussions with our group that includes Connie Houlden and Dolores Duncan, plus my own reading and reflections, I increasingly shifted to more right brain thinking.

My career development and retirement planning associates have been invaluable in providing input and feedback as I developed tools, exercises, and wrote over the many years of development from the initial Retire to the Life You Design workshop in 1996. Thank you to Marilyn Berezowsky, IJ McIntyre, Kate Jones, Linda Wilson, and Colleen Reichrath-Smith (who also happens to be my younger daughter) for your continued valued thoughts. Thank you to Rein Selles for giving me the opportunity to work under his umbrella contract with Alberta's provincial government, facilitating workshops for its employees and that continues with my own contract and subcontractors today. Thank you to Patricia Lynch Ordynec who was my first mentor in the career development field. There are many other colleagues I have been privileged to work with and learn from, too numerous to name – you know who you are. Thank you all!

To all writers and speakers who have shared their wisdom with me, knowingly or unknowingly, and from whom I've learned.

To the members of the Calgary Chapter of the Independent Publishers Association of Canada (IPAC) who spurred me to believe I could finish the book when I had been stuck, and to Cristy Haydn who invited me to the first meeting I attended. To Cheryl Cottreau, also a member of IPAC, who so willingly allowed me to include her Bottom Line poem.

To the early reviewers of the manuscript who offered valuable suggestions. To Jo Parfitt who readily agreed to publish the book, claiming it needed to 'see the light of day'. Thank you to Ray Fortune who, when he retired years ago, confirmed for me that my work was needed. As do my Retire to the Life You Design associates who asked for and encouraged me to continue writing 'the book'. To my husband, Tom, go the biggest hugs and 'thank yous' as he inspired the beginning of this work and so patiently and caringly supported me in every way possible as I wrote. You are loved.

TABLE OF CONTENTS

PART I – SIX WAYS TO LOVE YOUR LIFE

Model: The Six Circles of Life – A framework to live a full, enriched, and personally meaningful life

Model: Retirement Dimensions Profiles – to know your blend of core needs, values, and most natural ways of being

Tools: Personal Values Clarification Tool – to prioritize what is important to you now

Retirement Dimensions Introversion/ Extraversion Tool – to know what fuels and drains your energy now and in the future

Tool: The Practical Practice of Being to nurture emotional and spiritual well-being, to live joyfully, and to cultivate wisdom

Tools: Identifying Your Own Response

How to Move from One Stage to the Next – to know hope

Two Ways to Practise Retirement

Tool: Contract with Yourself

APPENDICES

FOREWORD

Nell has been talking about this book for the past several years. She just had to find the time to write it – not easy for someone with her many interests, activities and training schedule. Her experiences, training, knowledge and the invaluable insights she has gained from leading her Retire to the Life You Design workshops have lead her to the point of creating this practical resource for crafting a meaningful future.

Let me start by saying this book is not what I was expecting – it is better than I had envisioned. Yes, I knew Nell would, undoubtedly, draw upon her own expertise in personality theory and apply it; she is, after all, an invaluable member of the 'dream team' who researched and developed the Retirement Dimensions™ component of the Personality Dimensions® system. What I didn't realize is that, while this book is focused on those who are looking towards retirement, or who are already retired, it is also a powerful compendium of applications for adults in all stages of life development. The topics, exercises and general advice would fit beautifully into any adult life skills, career search or career change programs. These same practical suggestions and exercises will assist you to understand yourself, recognize your needs, your strengths and values; promote general well-being and better health in addition to fostering good interpersonal relationships.

Often retirement is seen as retiring 'from' a position in the workforce. Nell's approach will help you explore what you are retiring 'to' and will help you to reframe how you think about work, and retirement from it, in a holistic way that packages it personally for everyone. The compelling stories of real life individuals provide helpful illustrations for each point.

It is a great pleasure to introduce a book that has taken shape from a desire to help others into the full expression of these pages. Read it, consider the exercises and find out what fits you – and what doesn't. Retirement can be a daunting prospect for many people. Nell will help you to recognize and understand your needs – and help you retire to the future that you design.

Denise Hughes, Publisher
Personality Dimensions®
Retirement Dimensions™
www.career-lifeskills.com

DEAR READER

Have you ever asked yourself these questions?

- ◎ What do I say when people ask, "What are you going to do when you retire?" beyond the traditional golf, gardening, grandkids, and travel answers?

- ◎ How can I live my life true to who I really am and what I want for me, not according to someone's or society's expectations of me?

- ◎ Who am I when I am no longer identified by my work role?

- ◎ In what ways can I stay active, productive and keep my vitality for living?

- ◎ How can I stay healthy as I age?

- ◎ What can I do to maintain my mental faculties?

- ◎ How can I make new social connections?

- ◎ What is most important to me at this stage of life?

- ◎ How can I live together in one home with my husband/ wife/ partner when we both retire?

- ◎ How do I stop myself from stagnating and to keep learning, growing, and developing?

- ◎ How can I give back to society?

- ◎ What difference have I made living my life so far? Is it too late to still make a difference?

- ◎ How do I keep contributing my skills and experience?

- ◎ How can I keep earning money when I'm 60+?

- ⟲ What if I never want to retire?

- ⟲ What if I need to keep working?

- ⟲ How do I get off the treadmill and live more simply, calmly, and peacefully?

- ⟲ When is it time for me?

- ⟲ How do I find joy and passion in my life?

- ⟲ How can I build a new routine?

- ⟲ How do I keep from getting bored when I'm not working full time anymore?

- ⟲ How do I create a legacy?

- ⟲ What can I expect to experience in the transition to retirement?

- ⟲ What will give my life new meaning and purpose?

- ⟲ What is missing in my life?

- ⟲ What do I do if I'm scared of retiring?

- ⟲ Where do I find answers to these questions?

You will discover your answers right here. With practical information, models, tools, exercises, and inspiring stories, you have found the guide to fill the blank pages of the next chapter of your personal life story.

THAT 'R' WORD

"It's a change, a refocus, it's not retirement!" exclaimed Donna, 60, at the beginning of a new entrepreneurial venture.

And right she is. The traditional meaning of retirement is to withdraw from work and transition into full time leisure.

That model of retirement no longer fits for many of us, at least not for the initial 10-15 years of this new and uncharted territory.

Expecting to live longer than previous generations, today's 60-80 year olds and older folks are interested in staying active. For more than half, this means wanting or needing to continue to work – but on their own terms. For others, it means expanding on or shifting into new interests and involvements.

So, if not retirement, what should we call this life stage we are in the process of inventing?

We could, like Donna, consider the words refocus, or reinvent, re-engage, renew, re-energize, or redirect. What about calling it something positive:

- the second half of life
- third quarter
- second or third act
- un-retirement
- renaissance
- longevity
- down-shifting

- sage-ing

- conscious aging

- positive aging

- re-careering

- encore career

- legacy career

All of these have been tried with good reasons and with limited buy in. It seems we continue to think of this stage in our lives as retirement even though its *meaning* has shifted.

I propose, instead, we use the 'R' word as an *indicator of a new source of income*. This source could be one or a combination of pension income, investment income, work income, an inheritance – the common denominator being adequate finances to be *free to choose* how we now wish to live.

Rather than changing the word to an unsatisfactory new one, let's continue to use retirement in the new sense – the freedom to choose – whatever it is you want or need for your own life.

We can simply think of retirement to mean *the next chapter of your life*.

That is the meaning in which I use retirement in my work and for the purpose of this book.

MY STORY AND HOW THIS BOOK CAME TO BE

From the very beginning, I was destined for multiple changes in my life that played out like a continuous adventure.

In fact, the story of my life could be called: *Nell Ventures Into New Worlds*.

The first major adventure started ten years after I was born in WW II-occupied Amsterdam, the Netherlands, when, post war, our family of six joined the early-50s wave of migration from Europe to Canada. In Calgary, I started grade five with only 'yes', 'no', and 'I don't speak English' as my English vocabulary. My first adventure involved learning to fit into a new culture and learning a completely new language.

After finishing high school, graduating from the University of Calgary, and marrying a fellow student, Tom, our adventures continued as a couple criss-crossing Canada 10 times with Tom's work in the public service. I am still grateful to have lived in some of the most beautiful places in the world and in World Heritage Sites such as Waterton Lakes National Park and Wood Buffalo National Park – each move offering the new challenge of finding my way in a tiny community, a small town, or a relatively large city. Our three children were born in Calgary, Jasper, and Ottawa.

I could have hated moving frequently, and it wasn't easy as I felt lonely when we first arrived in a new place, but being naturally curious, I embraced each move as an exciting opportunity for yet-to-be-discovered possibilities. I believed I would find or, if necessary, create what I needed in my life. I was open to trying those options that merged the needs of our growing family with my own evolving interests and the opportunities available in each location.

Four Golden Rules

After several moves I had discovered that my needs fitted into three main categories. From then on I used these categories to guide me to intriguing involvements wherever we lived:

1. **Physical fitness and wellness.** I tried everything from aerobics classes, swimming, curling, badminton, tennis, hiking, walks with a new friend, square, ballroom, and line dancing, circuit training, weight lifting, hiking, solitary walks in nature, yoga, meditation, and Tai Chi.

2. **Contributing to my new community.** This often meant volunteering at something. Like other parents, I became a parent volunteer at school and a Brownie and Guide leader. When there was no pre-school program in one small community, I started one for my three-year-old son and the other children in the area. Elsewhere I helped start a learning disabilities association chapter. I volunteered on numerous committees and diverse community service boards. With this experience I served as a board development instructor and the first president of a professional association that I helped found. And consistently, I volunteered to write the newsletters for the organizations to which I belonged. The rewards of volunteering proved to be much greater than anything I ever contributed. With each experience, I gained skills, confidence, and new friends, plus an unexpected feeling of belonging to the community where I was, at times, an all-too-brief resident.

3. **Activities just for me.** These were for fun or self-development. This was sometimes the same as #1 and #2 and often meant singing in a choir wherever there was one. Books were my constant companions. I also always enjoyed learning and discussing new ideas, theories, models, and tools. I enrolled in training courses such as early childhood education, business, adult education, computers, writing, personal development, career development, psychology, and Reiki. I attended conferences and seminars and continued informal learning venturing into newer-to-me worlds of spirituality, meditation, positive aging, creativity, and expressive art (for non-artists!).

4. **Paid Work** (I added #4 during later moves.) When each of our children was established in school and gradually became more independent, I was 40 and knew it was time for my own career development. I ventured into a new world of part-time work starting a small short-lived accounting business from home, coordinating a community-wide fundraising

campaign, designing and instructing college written communication courses, designing and facilitating career/life development and work search workshops for adults in a career transition, writing a popular self-help guide called *Change and Transitions*, and consulting on a publication called *Mid-Life Career Moves*. I feel hugely privileged to have met and helped to facilitate the career development of thousands of individuals of all ages and from all walks of life, cultures, and beliefs.

When Tom accepted an early exit package and did not know what he was going to do next, I used the theories, tools, and resources from the trusted career/ life development field I knew and loved so well to create the first Retire to the Life You Design© workshop. Tom was my first client. The workshop helped him discover a direction and options that suited him. He decided to train for and start a whole new career as a self-employed mediator. We decided to return to Calgary where we had first started life as a couple, where our aging parents lived, where we were closer to our little cabin retreat near the mountains, and where two of our three children and grandchildren soon moved as well.

That was almost twenty years ago. My work has continued to evolve and expand and now contains the custom-designed models and tools I created. Because of requests, I created a train the trainer program. Retire to the Life You Design© is used by a cadre of professional associates in Retire to the Life You Design© workshops, presentations, and coaching practices, all aimed at helping to guide more people in their quest to discover and live their own next best chapter.

The Lessons I Learned

Through my adventures into new worlds, I have come to view life as a journey, not a destination, and the second half of life as a new opportunity to live the life you love with purpose, meaning, and fulfilment, a view supported by expert theorists and thought leaders.

This journey does not need to be precisely mapped out and pre-planned *in detail.* What we do need is to stay true to the core of who we are – the values, needs, interests and passions that drive our direction and guide our choices off-road or on. In defining that direction, we can be free to choose and take action on specific opportunities that invariably show up, wherever we are and whatever our circumstance.

If we need or want something that does not yet exist, we can create it. If we don't know how to do something, we can learn it. We can ask for help. "Where there's a will, there's a way", my mother taught me. How true that has proven to be!

I am still learning as I continue to venture into worlds I could never have imagined – still in the same direction, sharing what I have learned, know, and love with you through these words.

My wish is to inspire you to start creating the next best chapter of your own life – *the story of living, and being, uniquely you!*

HOW TO USE THIS BOOK

There are two ways to read this book:

1. Read it for ideas, information, stories, examples and inspiration.

2. Use it as a workbook by doing any of the exercises that interest you.

I recommend you read chronologically as each chapter logically follows and builds on the previous chapter. Alternatively, you can choose to read *Chapter 1: The Six Circles of Life* and *Chapter 2: Be Who You Are* to understand the framework, and then skip around to other chapters that interest you.

The same goes with the reflection questions and exercises in each chapter. You can do all of them or select those that resonate most. Everything offered here is intended as a tool you can choose to use or not. Consider this book your toolkit. As with any toolkit, some tools and exercises will be more useful to you than others. The ones less useful to you may be the very ones most beneficial to someone else. Sometimes you don't know how helpful an exercise can be until much later, after you've had time to reflect on it.

One thing you'll find most useful is to get yourself a simple, personally appealing notebook dedicated to doing the exercises, to writing your thoughts and ideas and what comes out of the exercises. This is your *Retire to the Life You Love* journal, where you start to design your own meaningful future.

INTRODUCTION

You've picked up this book because you're starting to think about retirement, you're getting closer to the date, or you have already left your most recent work and are wondering what's next for you. Maybe you already retired once and are now looking for what's next in a second retirement. Keep reading – this book is for you!

Retirement is a major, significant life change and comes with a whole range of conflicting emotions – from excitement, to worry, to downright fear. That's because with our new longevity, we could be retired as many years as we've been in the workforce already – equivalent to a whole new career. There are no roadmaps for this life stage – we are venturing into a new, uncharted territory. Old theories on life stages had us believing we'd be in decline for five to ten or so years post retirement and then we'd die. So all we had to do was enjoy our hobbies and a life of leisure – a well-earned reward for a hard, often labour-intensive life.

Today, however, many of us are stepping out into the unknown for twenty, thirty, or more years post what we think of as traditional retirement age. The majority of us are not in labour-intensive careers anymore. We are active and healthy. We know there are new opportunities with the gift of longevity granted a whole generation of boomers – the largest demographic in history. Boomers, and a smaller number of pre-boomers, have already started to explore and act on the potential and the new opportunities available now and yet to be created by us. Boomers will continue as they have throughout their lives to forge significant change to how we view and live this new life stage.

Retire to the Life You Love was written with the express purpose of helping you to personally explore the process of living this stage with all the potential for enriching your own life, for creating new meaning and purpose, for living authentically, for making a contribution to society, for making a difference by having lived your own life journey, individually and, by default, collectively. You want to be pro-active about choosing a direction and taking action – to not sit on the couch and live through other people's lives. You want to start with your own personal intention to design the life you want to live, to start crafting your own meaningful future.

This is exhilarating stuff. There are so many options and so much potential. So, how do you go about it all? The models, tools, and exercises in this book are designed to act as your guide to exploring your options, to lead you to choices you want to consider and the actions you want to take. Do this for yourself. Discuss with people who are important to you *after* you've done an exercise alone. You are an individual first – one that is unique in your own special way.

Nell Smith

Creator and Founder, Retire to the Life You Design workshops, presentations, train the trainer

nell@retiretothelifeyoulove.com – I would love to hear your story
www.retiretothelifeyoulove.com

Disclaimer

All examples in this book are real people who may be somewhat, or a lot, like you. For most examples I use actual first names with the individual's permission. For those I was not able to reach to obtain permission, I use fictional names and at times fudged details so they could not be readily identified. All are an inspiration. Thank you from the bottom of my heart for being who you are.

PART I

SIX WAYS TO LOVE

YOUR LIFE

CHAPTER 1

THE SIX CIRCLES OF LIFE

"To thine own self be true"

William Shakespeare

You are the architect of your own life, the sculptor, the artist, the author. You get to design and craft it the way you want.

Just *how* do I go about doing that, you ask?
And where do I start?

This section provides the models, tools, and exercises to focus on retiring TO rather than FROM something. The focus is moving towards what's next for you.

When I created version 1.0 of Retire to the Life You Design, I was using predominantly left brain thinking in its design. In 2008 I had a sudden stroke of insight. I woke up knowing I needed to create a right brain model that reflected the holistic approach I was already using. The model needed an inner core with overlapping circles, not straight lines and square boxes. I rushed into my home office excited to start creating.

The Six Circles of Life was born – one circle at the centre, the **INNER CORE** of who we are, **overlapping and connecting with** five outer circles that **EXPRESS** who we are in the outer world.

Focus on retiring
TO rather than
FROM something.

The Six Circles of Life represents a lifetime of learning for this writer with over 70 years of life experience, much of it in a field where I was privileged to have the opportunity to help thousands of people plan their careers or their retirement life. It also reflects my personal journey of exploration and self-discovery and all the mentors, writers, and guides who have helped me on the way to greater insights and deeper wisdom. Use the Six Circles of Life as a framework for:

❖ A way of living your life **FROM THE INSIDE OUT**. The Six Circles of Life is a personalized tool, one that helps you choose options which fit who you are as an individual with unique needs and desires, values and strengths. It is a way to live your life in an authentic way with meaning, joy, and fulfilment as individual and unique as you are.

❻ A WHOLE LIFE APPROACH to TOTAL WELL-BEING. Your authentic inner self is reflected in your choices for work, leisure, learning, and health. It is about body, mind, and spirit; about brain and heart; about being and doing.

❻ CONNECTEDNESS. Life is not compartmentalized and this tool shows the connection and overlap of six aspects of being you.

❻ A PRACTICAL and SIMPLE guide you can use over and over again. Simple though it seems, it is based on solid research and trusted theories.

❻ A way of BEING and applied as DOING, taking action.

The Six Circles of Life

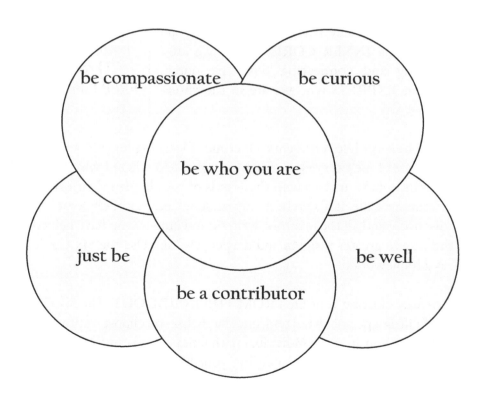

The Inner Circle

Essential to the framework is the inner circle connecting you to each of the outer circles:

- ⦿ **Be who you are** is your inner core, where you start and from which you get greater clarity about yourself and what is important to you unrelated to life roles. The inner circle is your guide to options in the outer circles. It is about understanding and prioritising what is important to you personally; about understanding and appreciating your innate temperament and strengths, those things that come most naturally and easily to you; and it is about increasing awareness of yourself as a spiritual being.

The Outer Circles

With enhanced insight into your authentic self in the inner circle, your choices in the outer circles become more clear, more intuitive. You can become more intentional about your choices knowing how these can fulfil your needs and enrich your life. The inner and outer circles guide you to live by design, not by default, guilt, or 'shoulds'.

The inner and outer circles guide you to live by design, not by default, guilt, or 'shoulds'.

- ⦿ *Just be* is about being and doing what brings you joy, happiness, and contentment – now or in the future. You could consider it a psychological/ spiritual bridge from the inner to the outer circles.

- ⦿ *Be well* is about creating physical and mental well-being.

- ⦿ *Be compassionate* is about developing and nurturing relationships – with yourself, family and friends, and society as a whole.

- ⦿ *Be a contributor* is about thinking beyond yourself – from me to we. To use and contribute your skills, knowledge, and wisdom in any

5

way you choose that contributes to the greater good of your family, community, or society.

🌀 *Be curious* is about stretching yourself, further developing your skills, your interests, or your knowledge.

Use the Six Circles of Life as a guide or roadmap to:

🌀 Live from the inside out – to being your authentic self, first.

🌀 Express who you are inside by your choices in the outer circles.

🌀 Choose activities in all five outer circles for *breadth* of experience and the life balance you desire.

🌀 Choose more activities in any one or two of the outer circles for *depth* of experience:

— for emotional and spiritual well-being – *just be*

— for mental and physical health – *be well*

— for social connections – *be compassionate*

— for meaning, purpose, and significance – *be a contributor*

— for cognitive health – *be curious*

Right here, right now, you are your future self in the making.

CHAPTER 2

BE WHO YOU ARE

"I already am,

I always was, and

I still have time to..."

Cheryl Cottreau

I met Cheryl Cottreau at a local meeting of the Independent Publishers Association. She shared a bit of her story with me and recited a poem that she had written about identity. It immediately struck a chord with me as I think it will with you.

Bottom Line

I am an accountant

I am a writer

I am an accountant

I am a writer and a poet

I am an accountant

I am a writer and a poet, a mystic and a muse

A teacher, a healer and an artist

A speaker and a leader

A counselor and a friend

I am an accountant.

If I am so many different things

With so many different talents

Why do I spend 50 hours a week

Being an accountant?

Because for now, the pay is better.

Like Cheryl, many of us identify who we are by a career or a job title – a source of income. Cheryl knows she is much more than that, but until she can access a new source of income her identity remains primarily an accountant.

What happens to that identity when you retire? Who are you then?

When I met Ron a few months after he retired, he showed me five different business cards he had created for the five projects he was newly involved in. Ron had continued to work part time. By continuing to do paid and volunteer work, he created five new identities.

It can be more difficult to know who we are when we stop working altogether or have been retired for many years. Julie called herself a CRONE – Creative Researcher of New Experiences – and even has a bumper sticker to prove it. Others have been equally creative in their search for a new identity.

This book is not about titles though. Titles are self-limiting. Why do we need to call ourselves anything? Even roles are self-limiting. Grandparent is high on the list of roles people gravitate to when they retire. Though this can be helpful to our offspring and rewarding for ourselves, it can also create pressure on our kids and grandkids if they perceive themselves to be the sole source of our happiness. Any one role in and of itself does not need to be the only involvement that fulfils us.

Let's expand what's possible way beyond the most obvious. Let's think in **and** out of the box!

Theories, Models, and Practical Tools

Philosophers from Plato to Aristotle to Meister Eckhart, more modern day psychologists such as Carl Jung, and today's thought leaders such as Deepak Chopra and Wayne Dyer have pondered the age old questions to understand who we are, why we are here, and how we are to live. Theories, books, and essays have been written and ideas proposed and debated.

What is clear from all is that we are human beings with **multiple dimensions – physical, psychological, cognitive, and spiritual.**

Based on the theoretical work already done for us, I like to create new or use existing practical tools that help us live the life we prefer now and in the future.

Building on Carl Jung's theory, for example, mother and daughter team Katharine Briggs and Isabel Myers created one such tool, the Myers-Briggs Type Indicator (MBTI), an internationally renowned and loved personality type tool. This psychological instrument sorts people according to a combination of preferences in four functions: source of energy, the natural way we perceive the world, the natural way we draw conclusions, and the degree of structure versus spontaneity we prefer in our lives. The MBTI helps us to understand ourselves and others and provides guidance in career/ life planning and effective communications.

Along with the MBTI came other personality and temperament tools such as David Keirsey's Temperament Sorter, Don Lowry's True Colors, Linda Berens' Essential Motivators Lens and Personality Dimensions™ and its specific application to retirement: Retirement Dimensions™ (Note: the trademark symbol is implied but not repeated in subsequent use of the name.)

Retirement Dimensions is a favourite tool of participants in our Retire to the Life You Design workshops. It gives us a good start in understanding who we are when not identified by a role or title.

Before you experience this helpful tool for yourself, please read the following explanation and introduction with tips for its use.

Important Introduction to Retirement Dimensions

Your personality temperament is based on patterns of inborn character traits. These are the genes of your parents and ancestors imprinted in your DNA. Each of us has an individual blueprint as unique as each individual snowflake or grain of sand. At the same time, each snowflake shares common traits that make snow, snow, for example, and not sand. So it is with people. Traits show up as a preferred way of doing things that are natural, easy, and form the basis of behaviours which are mostly unconscious. These behaviours can be called preferences – things we do without effort or thought.

To experience a preference, cross your arms across your chest. Notice which hand is up on the other arm and which hand is down. Now quickly do this the opposite way. You can do it, sure. Did you have to pause to think the second time? The first way is a natural preference and the second something you can do if you think about it first. The first is effortless while the second requires slightly more effort. The same is true for more significant preferences. Common traits and preferences are the basis of the Retirement Dimensions tool and are clues to four temperaments, identified in Retirement Dimensions by colours.

Colours have symbolic meaning. The four Retirement Dimensions colours were intentionally selected to represent character traits associated with this meaning so we can more easily understand the tool:

- ⊚ Gold is a symbol for tradition, stability, balance, and order.

- ⊚ Blue is a symbol for peace, harmony, and fellowship.

- ⊚ Green is a symbol for intellect and the power of the mind.

- ⊚ Orange is a symbol for energy and action.

The values exercise and the Profiles that follow will help to identify your personal, potentially best-fit Retirement Dimensions temperament and colour blend. These tools will enhance awareness of who you are and help to guide you to intentional choices in the outer circles.

Tips for Using Retirement Dimensions

- You likely have one colour that is most like you, supported by ones that are a lot like you, somewhat like you, or least like you. The combination of these four in the order you prefer them, is your individual blend of Retirement Dimensions and a beginning of knowing who you are in a number of key aspects of your life.

- Know that Retirement Dimensions is but one tool in a mix of many others you will find in these pages and elsewhere.

- Retirement Dimensions does not explain everything about you.

- You are a complex human being with multiple layers and dimensions – physical, psychological, cognitive, and spiritual.

- You are not one colour alone, but a blend, a plaid of colours.

Note: The Retirement Dimensions tool has seven sections to assess yourself. For the purpose of this book we will use a values clarification exercise to guide you to your potentially best-fit Retirement Dimensions Profile.

Personal Values Clarification Tool

Values are a key component of who we are. Values are our most important needs that help us navigate life. They are the hard drive of our personal operating system. We use them consciously or unconsciously when we make important decisions. They drive our direction and guide our choices, knowingly or unknowingly. Values are at the core of our being and indicate what matters to us more than anything else in the world.

Place a ✓ next to the 9 values most important to you:

☐ Stability and Regularity

☐ Facts and Frameworks

☐ Practical Solutions

☐ Duty and Responsibility

☐ Belonging   Total Organized Gold...

☐ Variety and Excitement

☐ Freedom and Independence

☐ Skill and Performance

☐ Action and Impact

☐ Spontaneity   Total Resourceful Orange..

☐ Curiosity and Learning

☐ Concepts and Ideas

☐ Knowledge and Competence

☐ Challenge and Innovation

☐ Intelligence   Total Inquiring Green...

☐ Authenticity and Personal Development

☐ Meaning and Purpose

☐ People and Relationships

☐ Ethics and Morality

☐ Harmony   Total Authentic Blue ....

Each value you checked is important! Use these values to help guide your direction and make decisions about options for your future.

Note the colour names of the two clusters with the greatest number of check marks. Then start reading the most-like-me and a-lot-like-me Profiles, below.

Retirement Dimensions Profiles

Source: Career/Life Skills Resources Inc.

Directions and Interpretation

The Retirement Dimensions Profiles are a snapshot of how your personality, temperament, and blend could live the next stage of life authentically. The Profiles were developed by a team, including a number of associates and myself, who have intimate knowledge of each of the colours and who walk the talk of their own colour blend:

- Start reading the profile of the highest total values cluster you checked in the Values Clarification Exercise.

- Then read the profile with the second highest.

- Use a highlighter, pen, or pencil to mark the word, phrase, or sentence that is true for you in each.

- Do not be concerned if every statement in any one profile does not apply. You are a blend of the four colours with one most like you, and others a lot like you, somewhat like you, and one least like you.

Organized Gold

Your core need is to belong through membership in a family, interest group or community. In retirement, therefore, you will find satisfaction in being of service to an organization you believe in. This may be a group that provides help to people in your community or in the global arena or it may mean taking a more active role in your family. Your need to feel useful and make a contribution may lead you to continue to do paid work in some fashion or to volunteer on committees or boards where your natural talents for planning, organizing, coordinating and stabilizing will be a strength.

As an Organized Gold person, you value stability, structure and a predictable routine. As you retire, you need to create your own daily and weekly routine including a number of regularly scheduled activities. You will enjoy joining a fitness group or other groups that share your interests. Because you find it difficult to relax until you complete a commitment, you may want to consider limiting the number of your commitments in order to create the balance you want in retirement.

The security and stability you have valued all your life now play out in wanting to continue to save money for a rainy day. Therefore you may find it difficult to spend money on yourself or on things that may seem frivolous until you are sure you can meet your financial obligations now and in the future.

Being responsible, you appear serious to others but you enjoy a good laugh like every other colour, though you usually prefer to have others tell the jokes.

In relationships you value loyalty, trust and respect. You show you care by performing acts of service for your loved ones. As an Organized Gold person, you take the lead in maintaining family traditions by honouring ceremonies and rituals established in the past or starting new ones. At this stage of life, you would enjoy collecting and organizing information on your family history and/ or other areas of interest.

Resourceful Orange

Your core need is to have the freedom to make your own choices. You want to do it your way. In retirement, therefore, you will find satisfaction in roles where your innovative, quick-acting, adaptable nature is a strength. You live in the moment and like to make it up as you go. Your ability to observe, assess, and come to a quick decision makes you a great trouble shooter in many situations.

As a Resourceful Orange person you value instant, fast-paced action. You are motivated by short-term projects with concrete results. If there is a competition or challenge involved, then it is even more enticing. You likely have a variety of skills and interests, which you enjoy pursuing alone or utilizing as a basis for your friendships. When retired you will find life an adventure in which you enjoy taking calculated risks. Whether you are involved in paid or unpaid work you will bring some fun-loving spontaneity to the role. Because having rules for the sake of rules is your biggest stressor know that to have a fulfilling retirement you need to be involved in activities which allow your optimistic, easy-going temperament a measure of free rein.

Since you love change, and live for the now, you might be tempted to make purchases on impulse. You find it fun to splurge, and enjoy being generous, often buying gifts for others. You only live once, and you would like to have the financial freedom to live life to the fullest.

Being someone with a quick wit you enjoy fast paced zingers. You laugh at outrageous situations, appreciate improvisation, and find original humour entertaining. You tend to be the one who impulsively tells jokes and funny anecdotes.

While you base friendships on common interests, you also choose to be around people who are fun and spontaneous. You may express your love of special people through surprise gifts and actions.

Inquiring Green

Your core needs are knowledge, competence, and innovation. You need to understand 'why?' and like finding answers and solutions on your own. In retirement, therefore, you will find satisfaction in furthering your intellectual understanding of existing concepts, or exploring new concepts, systems, or technology. You enjoy visioning, examining, and clarifying ideas.

As an Inquiring Green person, you value intellectual challenges and enjoy strategizing. You need to seek the core or root of complexities and likely will take a global view while continuing to think outside the box. You are passionate about searching out information and can easily lose track of time. You need quiet time to think and process the information you have accumulated. Because of your preference to be independent you may need to place limits on the time spent investigating on your own in order to seek out like-minded individuals for socialization; this will assist you in finding the balance you want in your retirement.

In retirement you will continue to gather the latest financial data and information to enable you to make informed decisions regarding your financial security. However, you will tend to postpone making financial decisions if you think that you do not have enough information.

You appear to others as a 'deep thinker' and possess a dry wit that leans towards sarcasm at times. People appreciate your ability to recall jokes long forgotten by others.

In relationships you value logic and objectivity which allow you to set your emotions aside. This approach has often led others to misunderstand you and to think of you as cold and unfeeling. However, you feel very deeply but sometimes have difficulty expressing those feelings. You continue to place high expectations on your relationships and need to be with people you respect. You show you care by spending time with those close to you and also spending time observing the interactions of others. At this stage in your life, you would enjoy researching areas of interests whether it is travelling to distant countries and investigating their histories and cultures or becoming involved as a volunteer in local community groups where your expertise in analysis is recognized and appreciated.

Authentic Blue

Your core needs are empathetic relationships and finding the meaning and significance that comes from having a purpose in life. In retirement, therefore, you will find satisfaction in getting involved with causes, things that hold a great deal of meaning to you either globally or locally – in roles where your warm, enthusiastic, honest and genuine nature are a strength. While you want to help make this a better world in which to live, you also enjoy taking time for the little everyday things that you find so fulfilling.

As an Authentic Blue person you value maximizing human potential – both yours and others. When retired, you will enjoy being involved in activities that allow you to stretch and grow to be the best you can be, while also inspiring and motivating family, friends, and perhaps even strangers to do the same. You would enjoy paid or unpaid work that provides opportunities for you to contribute as an imaginative, intuitive optimist. Because guilt is your biggest stressor, know that to have an enjoyable retirement you do not always need to fix everything in your world.

Since you empathize with and are very sensitive to the needs of others you will be tempted to make financial contributions to many worthwhile causes and find it difficult to choose among so many demands. You find it more difficult to spend money on yourself than on those who you feel need money more than you do.

Being someone who works at creating harmony, you may appear to be too nice, but you enjoy poking fun at yourself a little and will sometimes tell humorous stories, often at your own expense.

You are a people person. Having good relationships is vital to your enjoyment. As a natural nurturer you take the lead in creating harmony within your family and with your friends. In fact, you often put everyone else's needs ahead of your own as your way of showing support and encouragement. At this stage of life, you enjoy having the time to meet your friends' and family members' needs – whether large or small.

From your reading, write the colour name of the personality temperament that is:

Most like me ....

A lot like me ....

Somewhat like me ....

Least like me ....

The value of this tool is in honouring your true self, taking care of your core needs (that you may not even be aware of or have articulated), and choosing to live according to your authentic personality or blend of the four.

Many people in the workshops I facilitate gain significant insight from this tool and the validation of being and doing what is natural to them. They finally understand it is not only normal to behave the way they do but it is their strength. Roy told me this exercise gave him more clarity about who he was than 55 years of living had done. Each temperament has its own strengths – understanding and using yours can lead to contentment and fulfilment.

Each temperament has its own strengths

In relationships, use this tool as a conversation starter to develop a greater understanding and appreciation of the commonalities and differences each brings to the relationship. You may know your own values but does the significant person in your life know them? Remember, one personality temperament is not better than another. Each has equal value. Respect each other's natural way of being.

Pay particular attention to your core needs and values. In the past, these needs and values may have been met through work. When you retire or shift focus, you will need replacement activities to fulfil them. The five outer circles of the Six Circles of Life will help identify possibilities.

In *Appendix A*, in the *Be Who You Are* inner circle of the Six Circles of Life, or in your journal, record:

- The nine values you identified as most important to you in the Personal Values Clarification Tool.

- The core need(s) you identified in the first sentence of your Retirement Dimensions Profile.

- The natural strengths you highlighted in the Profiles.

In *Appendix B*, Color Your Circle of Self to illustrate your four colour blend as most like me, a lot like me, somewhat like me, and least like me. Do this in any way you wish and see what you create.

How You Display Your Temperament

An additional factor plays a key role in understanding yourself and others: the introversion/ extraversion factor. Your preference for the inner world of thoughts and reflection (Introversion) or the outer world of people and things (Extraversion) influences how you display your colour blend to the world. It provides clarity on the behaviours that either stimulate or drain your energy.

Retirement Dimensions Introversion/ Extraversion Tool

Source: Retirement Dimensions Toolkit – Career/ LifeSkills Resources Inc.

 For each of the nine paired statements, place a check mark beside the statement that best describes your preference *more often*:

1. More often

   ☐ I enjoy time alone or with one person

   ☐ I enjoy having other people around me

2. More often

   ☐ I keep my thoughts and feelings to myself

   ☐ I freely express my thoughts and feelings to others

3. More often

   ☐ I enjoy staying focused on one project at a time for lengthy periods

   ☐ I enjoy multi-tasking with several projects on the go at once

4. More often

   ☐ I prefer strangers to start conversations with me

   ☐ I naturally start conversations with strangers

5. More often

   ☐ I reflect first to prepare my response to a question

   ☐ I express my response almost immediately

6. More often

    ☐ I prefer others to initiate social engagements

    ☐ I prefer to initiate social engagements

7. More often

    ☐ I enjoy talking with one or two people at social events where I do not know people well

    ☐ I enjoy mingling with a variety of people at social events where I do not know people well

8. More often

    ☐ I prefer to take time-out from electronic communication tools such as email, social media, or smart phones

    ☐ I prefer to stay in constant touch with people through electronic communication tools such as email, social media, or smart phones

9. More often

    ☐ I enjoy deeply pursuing one or two of my interests

    ☐ I enjoy dabbling in several of my interests

How to Interpret Your Answers

The first checkmark in each of the nine pairs indicates a natural preference for introversion – energized by inner forces.

The second checkmark in each of the nine pairs indicates a natural preference for extraversion – energized by external forces:

- ℗ Behaving *in accordance* with your natural preference in each pair *gives you energy*.

- ℗ Behaving *out of accordance* with your natural preference in each pair *drains your energy*.

The *individual* preferences you checked are much more important than the total number of checkmarks. This is less about identifying yourself as an introvert or extravert and more about understanding your own and others' needs and behaviors *in each of the nine areas*. Use this tool as a guide to living a future that best fits who you are with those who share your journey.

You now have some of the key components of who you are, though of course there is much more to you. No one or two tools are sufficient. More will become evident as you continue your exploration of what's possible in the next chapters.

Remember Cheryl Cottreau, author of the *Bottom Line* poem at the beginning of this chapter? With an Authentic Blue personality (and a blend of the other colours) displayed as Introversion, she has lived through more than six decades of the exhilarating ups and debilitating downs that life presented her. Throughout, she wrote poetry and journaled as a route to feeling whole, complete, and happy with who she is.

Cheryl created this wise mantra to remind her of what is possible as she continues her life journey.

"I already am,
I always was, and
I still have time to..."

With the gift of longevity that science and healthy living has given us, we still have time and can continue to grow in spirit, wisdom, and our usefulness to society for many more years.

To prepare, start to Just Be.

CHAPTER 3

JUST BE

"From a place of stillness and contemplation, we can revision retirement... with extraordinary energy that transcends 'doing' in favour of 'being'."

Zalman Schachter-Shalomi

What on earth does Zalman Schachter-Shalomi mean by this *being*? What do I mean by this *Just Be* circle of the framework?

Let me first acknowledge the many people who have influenced me in this thinking – influencers living and dead, experts and guides, and people laying no claim to anything more than their own search for a deepening understanding of life.

One of my early influencers was, indeed, Rabbi Zalman Shackter-Shalomi. I found his book by chance while looking through a bookstore discount bin. On Reb Zalman's (as he is affectionately known) pages, I found what I myself believed to be true about aging and what he suggests could be a purpose for our increasing life spans.

Approaching sixty, Reb Zalman became increasingly depressed about aging's inevitable path to decline and demise. He gave himself a sabbatical to contemplate life after sixty. In the process he discovered a profound new vision of growing older explained in *From Age-ing to Sage-ing*, the book he published in 1995 and that spawned a whole sage-ing movement you can learn more about at www.sage-ing.org

In his contemplations, Reb Zalman came to the conclusion that getting older is not about decline after all. In spite of increasing wrinkles, creaky joints, and physical losses, he concluded aging is about personal and spiritual *growth*.

In Mitch Albom's non-fiction book, *Tuesdays with Morrie*, we read that Morrie, a retired college professor living with Amyotrophic Lateral Sclerosis (ALS also known as Lou Gehrig disease) in a rapidly deteriorating body, tells Mitch: *"Aging is not just decay, you know. It's growth. I embrace aging. It's very simple. As you grow, you learn more..."*

Just Be is about this growth in spirit. Spirituality simply means the conscious knowing that we are something more than our body and mind and that we are connected to a much larger universe. As our

Aging is about personal and spiritual growth

physical body declines, our spirit continues to grow in understanding, love, and wisdom.

Spiritual *growth* involves deepening the understanding of our own humanity, our place in the universe, and ultimately our usefulness in the universe – individually – and collectively as a generation.

This is the *gift* of longevity. This is the use of our *longevity*.

It is a hopeful thought, is it not? Instead of focusing on body decline, we can choose to focus on spiritual growth. We are after all, spiritual beings having a human experience. I'm not for one minute suggesting we neglect our physical bodies – indeed there are excellent ways to stay physically, mentally, and emotionally well discussed in the next chapters. These are all connected, though, so stay with me.

To start our own deepening awareness of spirit, Reb Zalman, Eckhart Tolle (*Awakening to Life's Purpose*), Carl Honore (*Slow*), Deepak Chopra (*Super Brain*), Osho (*Meditation for Busy People*), and many others encourage us to start by calming our minds and including contemplative practices in our lives. Strange as it sounds, it's really quite easy and calming, energizing and creative, playful and joyful. If you do not yet, you will come to love the practical practice of being!

The Practical Practice of Being

By *being*, we create the foundation for intuition, clarity and wisdom to enter our consciousness – when new insights occur as aha moments. Expect these 'aha' moments to increase as you adopt the practice of being.

Sometimes we need a catastrophic event to 'get it'.

A stroke of insight

Ironically, soon after reading Jill Bolte Taylor's story in her book, My Stroke of Insight, *I had a tiny stroke of insight myself. I had a brain bleed in a small area of my brain causing my inner GPS function to fail for a short time. During the subsequent healing process, I introduced into my life many of the ideas I share with you here to' just be'. Through being, I restored energy and gained new insights, including the moment when the Six Circles of Life framework was born.*

I don't recommend you wait for a whack on the side of the head to start this practice yourself. Just introduce any of the ideas in this chapter to start your own process to a deeper awareness, knowing, and understanding.

By practicing being, you create space for you – it is your turn now. This is the me time you want! You can start to feel calm again, reduce stress, and renew energy!

If this appeals to you, try any or all of the four practical practices to be still, be in nature, be creative, and be joyful. Understand for yourself how energizing and fulfilling it is to Just Be.

By practicing being, you create a space for you - it is your turn now.

Four Ways of Being

1. Be still. Be silent.

> **Inability to relax**
>
> *Getting close to retirement, Cody, a busy project manager in the oil and gas industry, was finally able to arrange his work schedule to attend one of my Retire to the Life You Design workshops. At the end of the day, Cody lingered behind to ask, "How do I meditate?" Cody told me his demanding job and stressful family situation contributed to high blood pressure and inability to relax. He knew he needed to take control of his situation. Meditation seemed a possible way to help him get there.*

Cody is not alone. In most of our hectic lives, we need this. We crave it. We know we need to calm the noisy traffic of the mind.

Did you know that *silent and listen* have exactly the same letters in them? Being *silent* allows us to *listen* – to be aware, to be conscious that we are not the mind. It allows us to be in the present.

Meditation is one way to be in the present. It is as simple as breathing. Since the breath is always with us you can do a restorative breathing exercise in less than one minute, anywhere, anytime, at work, riding public transit, waiting in line, waiting for someone, waiting for your tablet to boot up, waiting for your kettle to boil, before you get up, before you go to sleep. It's a mini-vacation from the thinking brain.

Try this. Sit, stand, or lie comfortably. Lower and soften your gaze or close your eyes. Focus your attention on your breath. Notice it going in through your nostrils, follow it down to your belly, then slowly back up to your nostrils and out again. Breathe deeply like this three times. Then breathe normally again. You can do this for longer, too. Try five and increase to 15-20 minutes as a good practice. Alternate three deep breaths with two normal breaths. When a thought enters your mind, just watch as it passes through and allow it to leave again, like a cloud passing by.

My great-granddaughter demonstrated what her pre-kindergarten class was taught to do when they get upset. She held up one clutched hand close to her nose to 'smell the flowers' and then held the other hand palm up to her mouth to 'blow out the candles'. Such a simple, calming breath exercise even a four-year-old can understand and do.

☉ Yoga combines stretching poses and breathing meditation.

☉ Tai Chi combines a moving form of yoga with meditation.

☉ Prayer is a form of meditation.

☉ Music – any type that is calming and feels good. Try classical music and mantras set to music. As I write this, I'm listening to Liona Boyd gently playing her guitar.

☉ Drum circles. Drumming is silent meditation to a beat. The drum vibrations go straight to your core, calming, healing, and energizing in a restorative community. Ditto for Tibetan singing bowls. Literally feel energy vibrations enter your being.

☉ Swim or run. A runner's high is a meditative state. Swimming, too, and any solitary activity that puts you in a state of flow.

☉ Contemplation. Be still and ponder your thoughts, an inspiring book you read, a movie or documentary that moved you, a meaningful conversation you had, a lecture or seminar that stimulated your thoughts.

"What we plant in the soil of contemplation we shall reap in the harvest of action."
Meister Eckhart

☉ Journal. Process your thoughts, feelings, and reflections in writing.

◉ Be in the present by engaging one of your senses with the aromatherapy of essential oils, freshly baked bread, or buttered popcorn; the taste of a cup of tea sipped mindfully; an exquisite piece of chocolate slowly melting in your mouth; the sight of a flickering candle flame; the visualization of your own special, sacred place; the sounds you hold dear; the magical healing touch of a big hug or a massage.

◉ Gratitude. Each day take a few moments to be silent and still to shift your thoughts to a little act of kindness, a conversation with a stranger, the beauty you see in nature – any little or big thing for which you are grateful.

Karen's insight

"The turning point that led to my deep happiness and things always working out for me was when I chose to begin each day looking for the miracles: the bird by my window serenading me to open my eyes, finding that very object that seemed to be lost forever, the person with that sparkle in their eyes, beautiful smile, and a song of good morning on their lips, that painted sunset that colored my heart with joy, and just the right person at the right time that crosses my path. Choosing to witness miracles connects me to the joy of life."

The past is history.
The future is a mystery.
The present is a gift – that's why it's called the present.

Write one or more practices you would like to gift yourself to be in the present.

....

....

....

2. Be in nature

We absolutely need nature, especially now as an antidote to the unnatural high-tech world we live in.

In *Boom, Bust, and Echo*, David Foote notes the five fastest growing activities we enjoy as we get older: walking, gardening, golfing, bird watching, and resting – the first four all outdoor nature activities.

Nature provides all that's necessary to Just Be. Nature connects us to the universe. All it takes is to consciously notice – to see, hear, smell, taste, and feel it.

- Research studies point to four elements that are particularly energizing to our being: water, trees, sand, and mountains. Get yourself outdoors to experience one or more of them. Allow yourself to be fully in their presence. Consciously notice what you see, hear, smell, or feel.

- Parks – experience the natural environment here. Growing up living in a city apartment in my early years, my mother regularly took my brothers and sister and I to a city park nearby. I loved being outdoors in nature then and now. In Calgary we chose to live minutes from a provincial park with walking trails, trees, grasses, mountain views, and a creek. At our remote, rustic cabin retreat near a mountain considered sacred by First Nations people, I experience what I call the Six S's: solitude, silence, simplicity, sun, sleep, and serenity – a spiritual place where I restore my energy.

- Gardens. Sit and listen to the sounds. Smell. Notice colours and nature's intricate design in a flower, a leaf, a tree, an insect. Enjoy an indoor plant the same way, year round.

- Waterfronts. Rivers, lakes, oceans. Listen to the sounds of the surf or the babbling brook. Watch the rhythm and flow of water. Feel the mist of the ocean spray and the sand between your toes.

- Anywhere. Taking a stroll anywhere outdoors will get you closer to nature. The trick is to notice your surroundings – see, hear, smell, and feel the air, the wind, the sun, the rain, the snow on your face. Look up at the sky and the clouds. Look down to the ground. Notice colours and shadows. Listen for bird song.

Which of these ideas or your own ideas do you want to include to be in nature?

....

....

....

3. Be creative

"We need now to be a more enriched human being, three dimensional. I call them the three C's, just like the three R's – the first C is consciousness, the second C is compassion, the third C is creativity. Consciousness is being, compassion is feeling, and creativity is action. We need all three simultaneously or something is missing,"

Osho, *Creativity, Unleashing the Forces Within*

"But I'm not creative," I already hear you say. I believed this myself and have learned over time that we are all creative in our own way. We may not make a living through art or call ourselves artists, but there is a creative spark in each of us that is begging to be expressed in any number of ways.

Gene Cohen M.D. Director of the Center of Aging, Health, and Humanities at George Washington University, did the first study showing that regardless of ability, participating in creative activities has a positive effect on physical health, mental health, and social functioning in older adults. The outcome of the creative experience is not important. The process is. Let go of the idea of being perfect and experience the gifts of imperfection.

> *The outcome of the creative experience is not important. The process is.*

- Writing. Is it any surprise this popped up first in my mind? I don't mean to suggest we should all write a book or a poem, though you may enjoy giving that a go. I mean any form of putting your thoughts into words. Journaling is one way to do this. Write your feelings and thoughts in a free flow style without judgment or editing.

- Write your own life story just for yourself or for your children and grandchildren, nieces and nephews. Yes, you have a story to tell!

- More storytelling. Share anecdotes and personal experiences with your family and friends. Create stories. Tell other people's stories or your own as a presenter or professional speaker. Try stand-up comedy or improvisational theatre.

- Photography. Capture the images and design you notice in nature, the people you are drawn to, the beauty that surrounds you. You'll see the world in a new perspective.

- Crafts. Designing or creating a craft in any medium – fabric, yarn, wood, china, glass, paper, precious metals, gemstones, clay, dirt, plants – use what appeals to you. Allow yourself to play and create.

- Dance. Express yourself with your whole body. Put on some music and give yourself permission to let go and move as the music suggests. Dance joyfully. No one is watching.

- Music. You already own a musical instrument – your own voice. Sing alone when no one can hear you (like you do in the shower) or sing along with others. Feel re-energized. Pick up that musical instrument you learned as a child and enjoy it now. Learn to play a new musical instrument for your own pleasure.

- Drama. Do improvisation and act in the moment. Tell a story or joke in a dramatic way. Try stand-up comedy. Musical theatre combines acting and singing.

- Art. Doodle – try doodling zentangles www.zentangle.com, creatively filling in open art or lettering spaces with doodles like lines, zigzags, circles of all sizes, dots, spirals, or chevrons. Sketch. Paint. Color mandalas – sacred geometric designs. Google mandalas and print one you like. Put on some calming music and color to your heart's content.

- Don't strive for a perfect outcome – just enjoy the process and the surprise you create.

- Design and innovation. Use your own ideas to design or create a framework, a model, a theory. Design and create a tool, a layout, an interior, an exterior. Create your own way of doing things. Build a better mousetrap. Lose yourself in the activity.

- Create a collage of words, phrases, images, and/ or quotes that are meaningful to you and find online or in magazines. Go to www.soulcollage.com to hear and see how to use images, intuition, and imagination to create a deck of cards with deep, personal meaning. Create your own gift or greeting cards using images, photography, and quotes. Phil Minnaar went so far as to create a whole dictionary of words, *The Positive Dictionary*, with only those words in the dictionary he perceived to have positive messages. What a creative project that must have been for him.

- Memory Books. These combine design, photography, writing, and preserving your memories. Create a hard copy or ebook using templates or your own unique ideas and designs. Be as simple or elaborate as you wish.

In what specific ways would you like to experience a creative activity?

....

....

....

4. Be joyful – play

"Joy is the keen poignant awareness of all that is buoyant and good in you. Joy increases as it is recognized, honored, and embraced. Joy calls us to aliveness, awareness, and health."

Jean Houston, online course, *Awakening to Your Life Purpose.*

En-joy all that is buoyant and good.

Joy is a keen pleasure, a gladness, elation, bliss. Joy is play, laughter, and fun. Joy makes us feel alive in the moment!

The joy of cooking

For Frank, everything about food and cooking is fun. From reading cook books to adjusting recipes, searching out just the right ingredients, seeing, touching, smelling, anticipating, and finally tasting and sharing the food, cooking is pure bliss.

What in your present life gives you that keen feeling of pleasure and aliveness?

....

....

....

What in your past have been joyful pleasures? How do you play? Think of your younger self and what gave you pleasure in early childhood, youth, early adulthood, mid-life – in any area of your life.

....

....

What joyful experiences would you like to include in the future? Ideas from the past, present, or in the *Be Still, Be in Nature*, and *Be Creative* practices will provide initial clues. Other clues will come as you continue reading this book and in the Interests, Skills, and Activities Sampler in *Appendix C*.

....

....

If nothing came to mind in the past or the present, know that you can create joy in the future. The practical practice of being is a path to discovering joy. Be curious and keep reading for many other ideas. Record your initial ideas in the *Just Be* circle in *Appendix A* or in your journal.

Bottom Line

Just Be practices allow inner space for calmness, clarity, intuition, and wisdom to enter our being.

Just Be is permission and freedom to live with integrity, being your authentic self.

Hit the pause button and create the essential space for this to happen naturally. This is *me* time. You are worth it. You deserve it. You need it.

The practical practice of being is a path to discovering joy.

Read on to know how *Chapter 3: Just Be* is related and connected to *Chapter 4: Be Well*.

CHAPTER 4

BE WELL

"When you think about aging, the two most critical elements are the ability to move the way you want to and the ability to think the way you want to."

Timothy Church

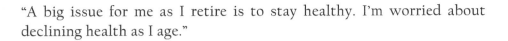

"A big issue for me as I retire is to stay healthy. I'm worried about declining health as I age."

This concern is repeated in every one of our Retire to the Life You Design workshops.

Like decade birthdays, retirement signals the realization that we are indeed getting older in years. Most other times we can forget about that galloping number but here it is facing us again. It sinks in that we are indeed in the second half of life, or the third or fourth quarter. We wonder, *what could be waiting for me down the road? Is a gradual decline to poor health inevitable?* That is the fear, isn't it?

Having made it to midlife already, we can expect to live, on average, into our 80s with many into the 90s, and those over 100 the fastest growing demographic in the world! You probably know people in their 80s, 90s, or 100s. Could one or more be a role model for how you want to age? Think for a moment of such a role model, living or dead. Perhaps a public figure comes to mind? If this is difficult right now, start looking for role models in the news or those you meet.

Your Role Models for Aging Well

Write here those people, living or dead, known to you personally or public figures, who you consider to be role models for aging well:

....

....

....

It's difficult for me to choose just one example – there are so many known to me. In my Tai Chi class, for instance, we have at least eight women in their 80s and one who's 90, most coming to Tai Chi even in the worst snow storms driving their own vehicles. Even our instructor is well into her 80s and lives an active life teaching two classes a week, attending instructor development classes and weekend workshops, volunteering with her church and her professional association, and travelling the world.

Hazel McCallion, the feisty former mayor of Mississauga, in Ontario, Canada, retired at 93 after 36 years in the position. Public service is her true passion. Harry Bernstein, author of *The Invisible Wall* and two further memoirs that continue his story, wrote his first book at 93 and considers his 90s the best years of his life. Olga Kotelko at 95 runs, jumps, and throws discus, shot put, and hammer, winning world class competitions. She says she feels as if she's 50.

In this chapter I will share common sense practices to live our *gift* of longevity with the long health we want.

Based on five thousand separate clinical studies, the Reader's Digest in its book, *Long Life Prescription*, concludes that:

- Illness is not inevitable.

- Damage can be undone – the neuroplasticity of the brain is a most hopeful discovery!

- Good health is a choice you make, not a pill you take.

- Good health includes happiness.

- Good health feels great.

- To be healthy years from now, choose to be healthy today.

- Choose to be healthy today with the Be Well Pyramid as your guide.

....

To be healthy years from now, choose to be healthy today.

The Be Well Pyramid

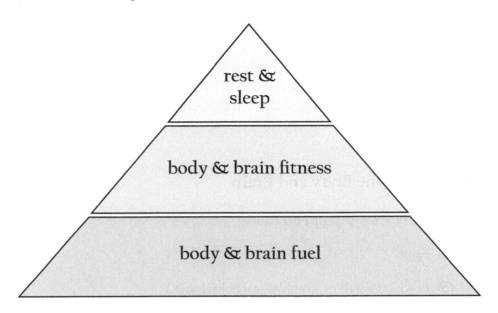

Body and Brain Fuel

Food and beverages are the body's fuel.

As with a car, the type of fuel we choose to put in it determines how our engines run. Should we use gas, diesel, electricity or a hybrid? What happens if we put sugar in the gas tank? How will it run then? For our bodies, should we eat animal or plant-based protein or a hybrid? What kind of carbs should we eat? What happens if we eat too much sugar? What about alcohol and caffeine?

We know we can't run on empty, but the daily choices of what to eat can be overwhelming, especially when information on what's in and what's out keeps changing.

The fuel question is what, when, and how much?

The information in this book is intended for a general reader, not those who have specific health concerns or dietary restrictions that require personal advice from a health professional.

I have come to trust these practical tips, assimilated from the unsponsored health and nutrition research published by the independent, non-profit consumer health group, The Centre for Science in the Public Interest, www.cspinet.ca

Tips to Fuel the Body and Brain

1. Use the Five F's as your Fuel Guide:

    ⊚ Fruit

    ⊚ Fibre (vegetables, complex carbohydrates)

    ⊚ Fats

    ⊚ Fish

    ⊚ Fresh options 80% of the time

2. Divide your plate in two halves:

    — One half is vegetables – think the colours of the rainbow and use a variety. Looks appetizing, too.

    — The other half is divided again, with one half protein such as legumes (e.g., beans, lentils, chickpeas), fish, dairy, nuts, or lean unprocessed meat (the size of a deck of cards or the palm of your hand), and the other half complex carbohydrates such as brown rice, quinoa, couscous, whole wheat pasta, barley, potatoes, or corn.

3. Eat until you are 80% full. It takes 20 minutes for the brain to get the message that we're full. In Japan, centenarians say *'hara hachi bu'* before each meal – *'eat until you are not hungry'*. By eating mostly plant based food

slowly and mindfully until not hungry, centenarians are lean. We can be, too.

4. Don't skip breakfast – you need fuel to start your engine. Think oatmeal and fruit plus a protein.

5. Fibre is essential for our guts to function well – vegetables, fruit, whole grains, and nuts.

6. Include vegetable oil every day – from 2 teaspoons up to one tablespoon (5-15 ml)

7. Drink water most of the time. Herbal or green tea is good too.

8. Drink a cup or two of coffee to stimulate your brain.

9. Drink a glass or two of red wine a day as an antioxidant and enjoy sipping.

10. Eat an ounce or two of good quality dark chocolate every day as an antioxidant, my favourite practice!

11. Eat a handful of nuts for brain food – walnuts are even built like the two halves of the brain.

12. Vegetables, berries, nuts, and seeds are power foods for every cell of the body.

13. Lose (or don't gain) excess weight, especially around the middle.

14. Brush your teeth, and floss, daily to help prevent plaque from building up and entering your blood stream.

15. Don't smoke.

Several health conditions you can help prevent as you age, or control if you already have them, include hypertension (that can lead to heart disease and stroke), Type II diabetes, dementia, and many types of cancer. Type II diabetes is in danger of becoming an epidemic for our generation if we don't stop it now. Excess weight is a precondition that hastens the onset of all of these health concerns. Use:

- The DASH Diet (Dietary Approaches to Stop Hypertension) or OMNI diet to help lower blood pressure and cholesterol without medication.

- The Diabetic Diet to help regulate insulin and sugar in the blood.

- A lifestyle plan such as Weight Watchers® to help lose excess weight and maintain a lean body. Practise putting down your fork between bites and chewing very slowly.

- Use these 15 tips, plus the fitness tips, rest and sleep for long health.

Researchers have studied global pockets, known as the Blue Zones, that claim the largest concentration of people aged over 100: Ikaria, Greece; Nicoya, Costa Rica; Okinawa, Japan; Sardinia, Italy; Loma Linda, USA.

Are you curious about what they found were centenarians' secrets to longevity? They:

- Eat mostly a plant based diet.

- Have low-intensity exercise built into their daily lives.

- Take time to slow down, rest, relax, and recuperate.

- Participate in a spiritual community.

- Spend time each day with like-minded people they care about.

- Live with family as their top priority.

- Live with a purpose that is pursued every day.

- Don't smoke.

Kamada, an Okinawa centenarian, gives us this advice *for long health*: "Eat your vegetables, have a positive outlook, be kind to people, and smile."

Body and Brain Fitness

"When you think about aging, the two most critical elements are the ability to move the way you want to and the ability to think the way you want to."
Timothy Church, professor of preventative medicine at the Pennington Biomedical Research Center and co-author of *Move Yourself.*

I think most of us agree with Church: we want to retain our mobility and mental acuity.

His key advice for both: Move more, sit less!

All body parts, including the brain, need blood to fuel each cell. Moving the body helps the heart to pump and the blood to circulate to each cell, a rather essential function for good health.

Centenarians in the blue zones build low-intensity exercise into their daily lives. We can, too, by remembering to move more – sit less, even a little! Every health and fitness study points to the danger of in-action and dis-use of body parts and the benefits of more movement of whatever type. An inactive life style will bite us later if we don't start moving now.

    ⦿ Moving more can be as simple as adding **N.E.A.T.** to our day – *Non Exercise Activity Thermogenesis.* Any physical activity that isn't a structured, purposeful exercise is NEAT. NEAT can account for anywhere from 15 percent to over 50 percent of daily energy expenditure. NEAT activities can be cooking, cleaning, gardening, puttering, emptying the garbage, tidying a room, taking the stairs, and walking, not driving to the store. Every chance you get to practise NEAT, take it. If I have 15-30 minutes, I ask myself, "Shall I check my e-messages or go for a walk? Shall I drive to pick up that tub of yogurt or walk to the store?" When I'm wise, I go for the walk.

    ⦿ The majority of people I meet on my walks have a dog. It's not uncommon for them to tell me, "If it wasn't for my dog, I wouldn't be out here!" You wonder, aren't we as deserving of movement as our dogs are? A few people I meet foster rescue dogs and walk as many as three at a time. One walks three different dogs three times a day. That's nine walks a day. So, if this is what it takes to get you moving, own, foster, or borrow your neighbour's dog to walk. Of course dogs are much loved for themselves as loyal companions and not only as movement motivators.

◉ Church's research, and the research of others, suggests that exercising five times a week for 30-60 minutes (the minimum recommended) and then be done with moving the rest of the day is not good enough. We need to build in movement throughout the day. Get a pedometer (or download a free app) and aim to walk 10,000 steps a day through every type of movement.

◉ Some enlightened offices now have standing desks and treadmills with computers so you can do your work walking.

◉ Sit on an energy ball instead of a chair and strengthen core muscles. Do a few stretches while on the ball. Watch a favourite TV program while walking on the treadmill. We need to get even more innovative on how to build movement into our daily activities.

◉ Do some leg lunges or arm stretches while waiting for the coffee or the microwave to do its thing. 'Write' the letters of the alphabet with each foot and hand by rotating the ankle and wrist. Build flexibility into daily life.

◉ Grow your own vegetables or herbs. This provides the double whammy of exercise with a fresh market outside your door. Some restaurants are doing this already and the roofs of some high rise buildings have gardens – they're on to something. This is also what the centenarians in the blue zones do out of necessity. Even at 104, some of them are out there with a hoe, weeding and harvesting. The results can't be disputed.

◉ Do strength training, too – twice a week. Use resistance exercises like lifting weights to build muscles, to support the spine, to prevent falls, to continue to function independently.

⊚ Have fun. We need movement to be fun, too. Go dancing. Participate actively in any sport – don't just be a passive observer. Want to give Zumba a try? Aquasize? Disc golf? Geocaching? Tennis? Bowling? Pickleball? Any movement with a fun factor will motivate us to keep doing it. If it involves another person or a community of like-minded people, so much the better.

Do any one or all of these activities for variety.

Just remember one thing:

....

Move more — sit less — even a little!

More tips for brain fitness

"Neuroscientists have found that those people who use their brain more often, on the job or at play, seem to possess brain saving reserves. They believe that stressing the brain in ways similar to the way we stress muscles during exercise produce similar benefits – a stronger, fitter, more flexible brain."

Source: Long Life Prescription

Here's how. (Do these in addition to moving more and sitting less.)

⊚ Keep working – paid or volunteer – full or part time – see *Chapter 6: Be a Contributor.*

⊚ Keep learning – formal or informal – see *Chapter 7: Be Curious.*

⊚ Keep socially connected – see *Chapter 5: Be Compassionate.*

⊚ Stress your mind in instant, positive ways:

— Switch hands to brush your teeth, write a list, or stir a pot.

— Do cross-body movements – wave arms from one side of the body across to the other. Kick legs in the opposite directions like the cancan dance.

— Add or multiply numbers in your head. Count backwards silently or out loud.

— Say the names of family members backwards (Norman becomes Namron, for example).

— Read these sentences backwards. Read a whole paragraph backwards.

— Balance on one foot, then the other. Focus your attention on a spot in your view.

◉ Challenge your brain every day through:

— puzzles

— reading

— thinking

— problem solving

— conversing

◉ Play games such as card or board games.

Rest and Sleep

Each of us has a natural pace that suits our energy level, physical condition, or preferred lifestyle. For you that pace may be more or less active or relaxed than your partner, neighbour, co-worker, or friend.

What suits your natural energy level, physical condition, needs, and preferred lifestyle?

🌀 Go-go – active pace?

🌀 Slow-go – relaxed pace?

🌀 No-go – resting pace?

In the first years of retirement to the early, mid or late 70s, people generally want to stay active at their own pace. Gradually (or more abruptly as the result of a health concern), they naturally start to relax the pace. When they're no longer physically or mentally able to function independently, they reach a no-go or resting pace.

What balance of pace do you prefer at this stage of life – all go-go or all slow-go, or a blend of the two? You can choose, for instance, to not rush through everything, to slow the overall pace a little if you wish. Or to start including a few slower paced activities you identified in *Chapter 3: Just Be*. Some relaxation is necessary. You can also choose to let go of one or more of your energy-draining involvements and start new, more energizing ones. On the other hand, if you have more energy than you actually use, you can become more or differently active. Learn how in the following chapters.

To restore, maintain, and improve health, include Just Be, better fuel and fitness, and adequate rest and sleep practices as part of daily living.
I think we all know in our heart what our bodies and mind need, if only we will listen and take action.

Sleep

Adequate, restful, sleep is imperative for long health, so finds just about every health and wellness study. Like a battery, we need to regularly recharge the energy we use during the day. Sleep is our recharger.

So what is *adequate* sleep and how do we get it?

If you have insomnia, these questions are not fluffy. If you only occasionally have trouble sleeping, you can skip this section and be thankful!

Studies estimate that at least 10% of the population have chronic insomnia while up to 55% have periodic insomnia. The mind continues thinking even as the head hits the pillow. Some people fall asleep just fine but then wake up during the night and can't get back to sleep. Some have sleep apnea, a physical obstruction that interrupts and disturbs the cycles of REM and Delta waves we need.

Sleep specialist Stephanie A. Silberman, reports in the *Insomnia Workbook*, that a change in normal routines, such as an abrupt cessation of work, can be a source of insomnia.

According to Silberman, here's how to create good sleep hygiene if you have trouble sleeping:

- Set a regular sleep schedule and stick to it.

- Forget about a magic number of hours of sleep. Some people are short sleepers while others are long sleepers. Get the hours your body needs to feel refreshed when you wake up.

- What to do before bed:

  — Do relaxing activities for an hour or more before bed – deep breathing, meditating, non-stimulating reading, listening to music – anything that relaxes you.

  — Drink coffee only in the morning and not afternoons or later. Depending on your age and body, caffeine can take anywhere from 3-10 hours to metabolize in your system. Even if you can fall asleep easily, residual caffeine can cause you to wake up during the night.

  — Avoid alcohol before bed if doing so has you waking up feeling restless. Though it may help to fall asleep initially, sleep rhythm may be disturbed later on in the night.

  — Use your bed for sleeping. Don't read, watch TV, eat, talk on the phone, or use your tablet in bed. Do these in another room.

🌀 How to improve your sleep environment:

— If you work from home, have separate spaces for work and sleep.

— Use a comfortable bed and pillow.

— Keep your bedroom at a temperature that's comfortable for you – not too hot, not too cold – just right.

Restful, restorative sleep is possible. It's important to talk to a health care professional if these tips are not adequate for your personal needs.

Your Long Health Practices

You are likely already doing many things well. Are there ideas from the Be Well Pyramid or your own ideas that reminded you or suggested ways to have long health?

In the left column remind yourself of what you are already doing for long health.

 In the right column write what you want to start doing. Write in the positive present tense, as if you are doing it now. E.g., eating fruit and vegetables for snacks; walking 10,000 steps every day.

<u>Doing Already</u>   <u>Start Doing</u>

....

....

....

....

....

Record key ideas from both columns in the *Be Well Circle* in *Appendix A* or in your personal journal.

Be Well practices allow us to be and do what we most care about longer!

The body and mind are the vehicles for *Chapter 5: Be Compassionate*, and *Chapter 6: Be a Contributor*.

CHAPTER 5

BE COMPASSIONATE

"I believe that at every level of society – families, tribal, national, and international – the key to a happier and more successful world is the growth of compassion."

The Dalai Lama

To be compassionate is to be caring, kind-hearted, sympathetic, charitable, and humane.

Being compassionate is the path to cultivating and nurturing relationships – with ourselves, family, the friends and acquaintances we already have and want to keep, and those we have yet to meet.

Being compassionate is an attitude we can cultivate, nurture, and grow. It's a process worth embracing if you care about yourself, others, the community, and the world. And who doesn't?

The story of two wolves

One evening an old Cherokee told his grandson about a battle that goes on inside all people. He said, "My son, the battle is between two 'wolves' inside us all.
One is Evil. It is anger, envy, jealousy, sorrow, regret, greed, arrogance, self-pity, guilt, resentment, inferiority, lies, false pride, superiority, and ego.
The other is Good. It is joy, peace, love, hope, serenity, humility, kindness, benevolence, empathy, generosity, truth, compassion and faith."
The grandson thought about it for a minute and then asked his grandfather: "Which wolf wins?"
The old Cherokee simply replied, "The one you feed."

The one you feed.

I believe the wolf we most want to feed is Good. The Evil Wolf mischievously appears now and then begging to be fed too. When we recognize this Wolf for what it is, we can ignore it and focus on the Good Wolf instead. That focus, that intention for good, is what grows compassion. Growing compassion leads to building caring relationships with ourselves, others, and society as a whole.

Targets for Compassion

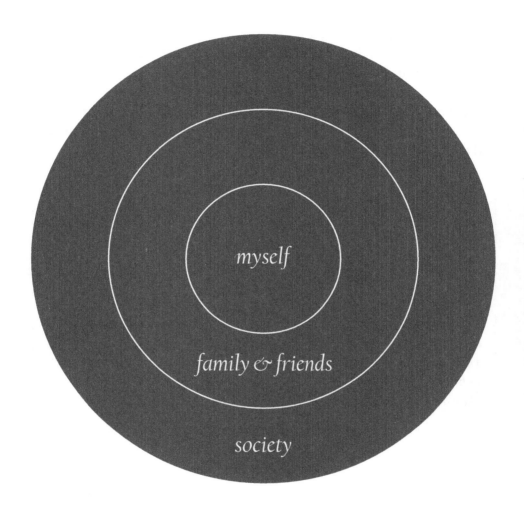

myself

family & friends

society

Myself

"How much we know and understand ourselves is critically important, but there is something that is even more essential to living a wholehearted life: loving ourselves."

Brené Brown, *The Gifts of Imperfection*

Target the bull's eye by being kind to yourself *first*. All too often, we think of ourselves *last*. That's only natural when we're focused on raising a family or building a career. Now it's our turn. It starts here, with ourselves.

You may have been taught that to be kind to yourself is selfish. It is so common to believe we are not as worthy as others, those others we now shower with our time, attention, and compassion. Guilt about being good to ourselves is particularly true for the Authentic Blue personality temperament. And we all have some of that Blue in us.

Let's agree to be a bit selfish from this point on. You'll see how this is the starting point for being compassionate with others and the globe.

Flight attendants instruct us all the time that in an emergency the oxygen mask goes on ourselves first, with the person in our care second. If we don't care for ourselves first, we will be the ones needing care next. Let's not wait for a catastrophic event to learn this.

Changing the Tape

Aren't we naturally our own worst critics? There is a constant voice playing in a looped tape, "Why didn't I say this, why did I do that, why can't I be more like... (fill in the blank)? I'm not good enough!" We compare, we criticize, and we're the undeserving recipients of much of this.

If we don't care for ourselves first, we will be the ones needing care next.

We can start to change the tape by accepting AND appreciating who we are for ourselves and to forgive

61

Your work is not your worth

ourselves for past mistakes. We've all made them – we just make different ones. Life continues to provide lessons – that's the business of living, learning, and growing.

Imagine for a moment that you have an inner bank account with a balance not of money, but of self-worth. If there is little self-worth in the account, we need to be very frugal with what we have. When we have a healthier balance we can afford to be more generous. Our account needs constant deposits, especially if we are big spenders. Big spenders with little self-worth quickly go into debt, and when in debt, get ill. A negative balance does not contribute to good health nor positive, caring relationships.

Up to now, you may have come to rely on work as a main source of self-worth. Work gives us status, respect, money, routine, social connections, and a sense of purpose. Upon leaving that work, you're in a quandary wondering, "Who am I now and what is my worth?"

Your work is not your worth, you may come to realize. Status, respect, money, and routine are what others decide to bestow on us, or not, if they so choose. These are **extrinsic** sources of worth. Look now for **intrinsic** sources. Your true worth is the essence of who you are untethered by roles and titles. Go inside first. Then start creating the relationships and social connections you are attracted to with a new sense of purpose.

"What I am looking for is not out there, it's in me."

Helen Keller

In *Chapter 2: Be Who You Are*, you identified your personal values, core needs, and natural blend of personality temperaments expressed through behaviours that create or drain energy. In *Chapter 3: Just Be* you explored the practical practice of being through silence, listening, and noticing; through the power of nature, creativity, and joy. You have already started the process of increasing intrinsic worth. Let us continue.

Do this exercise and the suggestions following it (especially the collage!), as a reminder of your personal strengths. If you believe some traits to be positive or negative, you'll be right. They are exactly what you believe them to be. Hint: they are neither positive nor negative; they just are.

Your personal strengths

Take the time to reflect, consider, and check all that apply – no minimums, no maximums. Be kind.

☐ dependable	☐ friendly	☐ positive
☐ patient	☐ humorous	☐ generous
☐ compassionate	☐ organized	☐ cooperative
☐ energetic	☐ calm	☐ committed
☐ honest	☐ resourceful	☐ independent
☐ efficient	☐ knowledgeable	☐ consistent
☐ ethical	☐ understanding	☐ discreet
☐ loyal	☐ competent	☐ cautious
☐ tactful	☐ respectful	☐ accurate
☐ entrepreneurial	☐ curious	☐ empathetic
☐ multi-functional	☐ practical	☐ kind
☐ enthusiastic	☐ trustworthy	☐ wise
☐ meticulous	☐ persevering	☐ analytical
☐ assertive	☐ spontaneous	☐ courteous

☐ outgoing   ☐ innovative   ☐ data-oriented

☐ punctual   ☐ contemplative   ☐ people-oriented

☐ ambitious   ☐ logical   ☐ ideas-oriented

☐ flexible   ☐ accountable   ☐ task-oriented

☐ tolerant   ☐ optimistic   ☐ detail-oriented

☐ self-starting   ☐ adventurous   ☐ result-oriented

☐ imaginative   ☐ strategic   ☐ action-oriented

☐ creative

5 Things To Do Next:

1. Add any strength you have that is not on the list.

2. Create a page to record just the strengths you checked.

3. Add the checked strengths to the *Be Who You Are* circle in *Appendix A*.

4. Create a word and/or picture collage of your personal strengths from images in magazines or online.

   — This is fun and more powerful than you might think. Try it and see for yourself!

   — Have a collage-making get together with friends.

5. Put your list or collage in a prominent place, such as a bathroom mirror, bulletin board, closet or fridge door as a daily reminder to appreciate your personal strengths.

A Special Note for Caregivers

If you are currently, have recently been, or are soon to be a caregiver, it is doubly important to remember you are worth care, too. Gift it to yourself. You are still you, an individual apart from the person you are caring for. You have worth and need love and attention, too. Rosalyn Carter famously said we all have been, are, or will one day be a caregiver or a care receiver. Let's build up our resilience for these roles now.

"Be your own best friend first before you tell the world who you are."

Diana Mitchell

Family and Friends

Research and anecdotal evidence suggest that most people, when they leave current work, miss the readily available social connections they had in the workplace. Unless you already have activities you share with colleagues outside of work, the likelihood of continuing these connections is slim. At best they are infrequent – unless you make a concerted effort to make it otherwise.

Mostly cut off from work, you may now expect your family and current friends to fulfil your social needs. And they can – to some extent. This may not be enough, though, as each may have created their own lives already without you being a big part of it. So it's equally important to build an additional network of friends. This is especially true if you move to a new location.

The following two examples illustrate two extremes of connections with family and friends.

Not so great opportunities

In a location many think of as a perfect place to retire, we attended a reunion and anniversary celebration of an organization from my husband's youth. We saw a couple sitting alone not talking to anyone. Since we had come on our own too, we seated ourselves across from them. After the preliminary memory sharing, I enquired about their current life. They had moved from a community, they said, with cold, harsh winters to the much warmer community close to the event we were attending. Smiling ruefully, they admitted, "We know all the channels on TV now". We learned they had not explored much beyond the four walls of their condo. Cut off from work and their old social network, they did not know how to go about meeting new people and were uncomfortable leaving their comfort zone. I was sad to hear their story.

I am even sadder to know they are not alone in their experience with isolation and loneliness. In Britain, this phenomenon has been well documented with one research study calling it a 'loneliness epidemic'. The study found that post 65, large numbers of British people are turning to alcohol and TV as their sole or main source of companionship. Britain is not alone experiencing this phenomenon.

There's less loneliness in Asian cultures where families live in intergenerational households and older people are respected.

Just doing it

At the invitation of one of her daughters, Nhuong, 76, a friend in my own Canadian community, lives together with her husband, daughter, son-in-law, and young granddaughter as one integrated household. They share some of the childcare and cooking and most of the celebrations and vacations. Nhuong has an individual life too, involved in organizing volunteers for several not-for-profit fundraisers, volunteering in her church, and singing in two choirs. Daily meditation is an essential part of Nhuong's being. She is one of the most generous people I know in her

> *consideration for anyone needing a kind word, a phone call, a visit, a care package, or a reflexology treatment. She has a practical 'just do it' attitude that is decidedly upbeat.*

These two examples represent the extremes of full *isolation from* family and community and full *integration with* family and community. Most of us likely live somewhere in between these two extremes.

 Where on this continuum do you wish to live your future? Place an X on the line closer to isolation or closer to integration.

Isolation ....Integration

If in the Introversion/ Extraversion exercise in *Chapter 2: Be Who You Are* you checked a greater number of the first statements, your X may be to the left of the middle. If you checked a greater number of the second statements, your X may be to the right of the middle. Respect whatever degree of social interaction fits with who you are.

To whatever degree, we all need positive relationships in our lives. And we need the tools to build and nurture relationships, including the relationships closest to us.

The Five Love Languages – for singles and couples

One helpful tool that makes perfect sense is Gary Chapman's *Five Love Languages*. In his book, Chapman introduces the idea that there are five love languages we use with one or more being our most natural way to express compassion and with one or two others being less natural. We feel loved when others express their affection in our own preferred way. Understanding our own and others' preferred language, and acting on it, is of huge benefit in building and nurturing relationships with anyone – men, women, children, youth, co-workers, friends – all those already connected to us and those we have yet to meet.

The Five Love Languages are:

- ℗ Words of Affirmation – words that express appreciation or encouragement

- ℗ Quality Time – activities you do exclusively with another

- ℗ Receiving Gifts – a visual symbol of affection you can hold in your hand

- ℗ Acts of Service – a helpful action that expresses care and compassion

- ℗ Physical Touch – an emotional expression of affection

These five are related to your personality temperament, too.

Inquiring Green personalities generally find it difficult to express appreciation and affection. They may say that, "I told you once that I loved you. I'll let you know when something changes." Done. They generally aren't the hugging types either. Their feelings are deep and genuine and more easily expressed through the other three languages.

Organized Gold personalities are generally service oriented so they most naturally like to do things for others. Likewise, they appreciate it when others do things for them.

Authentic Blue personalities generally express affection most easily. They may appear gushy with their words, gifts, and touch; know that these come from a genuine, not artificial place. They like to have affection expressed to them the same way.

Resourceful Orange personalities generally love to give spontaneous gifts. They delight in surprising others and receiving a considerate gift in return, small or large.

How to Use the Five Love Languages

1. Reflect and observe others' preferred love languages, especially those close to you – partner, parent, child, a friend. Know what makes you cringe a little on receipt. Receiving gifts graciously is something I've had to learn as it comes least naturally to me. A certain amount of guilt or not feeling worthy may be part of it. I have learned to avoid saying, "Oh, you shouldn't have". I now say "Thank you, this is lovely. I'll enjoy using it." Knowing the gift is an expression of appreciation or affection, we negate the intent with which it is given if we simply shrug it off. This does nothing for building and nurturing good feelings in relationships.

2. Know which is your own most natural way of expressing compassion. It may be that your kind act of service comes naturally but may not be noticed by someone for whom this is not preferred. A discussion on the five love languages could be helpful.

3. All of us need words of affirmation. "I really appreciate that you look after the maintenance in the house." "Your project turned out well! I'm really proud of you!" "You are so kind!" A simple, sincere "Thank you!" accompanied by a smile, does wonders. Use more of these all the time, even if at first it doesn't come easily. It can be practised and learned.

4. Quality time together can be demonstrated by being in the present with the person you're with. If you're having lunch with someone who's constantly texting another person or glancing at a TV screen, do you feel you have quality time with them? Not so likely. Eye contact lets another know you're with them. Doing any activity you both enjoy and being fully present is quality time.

5. How long does a caring touch linger in your memory? A hand held, an arm touched or draped over your shoulder, a hug? Touch is a necessity of life.

All of us need words of affirmation.

Rank the five love languages in your most natural order:

1. ....

2. ....

3. ....

4. ....

5. ....

What do you suppose is the love language of someone close to you – your partner, your child, your parent?

....

If you're not sure, change what you do now by trying a new language and see what happens. Once you're clear, use more of the other's language, in addition to your own. Your relationships will bloom.

An amazing thing happens when we show care and consideration for others. It's called the butterfly effect. Some call it paying it forward or random acts of kindness. One small action sets in motion a chain of reactions that reverberates from that person to another and then to more others, affecting people in ways we will never know.

Uncommon kindness

An almost unheard of example happened to me not long ago. When the key in my car would not turn to start it, I called the local dealership's service department. I got the assistant service manager on the line. When none of his suggestions on the phone solved my problem, he offered to come over during his lunch hour as I was not far away. When he arrived, he was quickly able to get my car started again. He would not even consider a tip for his help. That amazing service was above and beyond any of my expectations. His kind act made me feel great all day. At the drive through coffee shop, I paid it forward paying for the coffee of the person behind me. At Canada's own Tim Horton's coffee shops, I've been told by staff it is not uncommon for such an action to carry on before someone breaks the chain. Everyone feels great doing something for someone else. The good feelings last for a long time and translate into further feel-good actions, kind words, a smile, or a loving touch. Who knows how far this extends and how many people are positively affected?

With the five love languages in mind as a general operating principle, there are strategies that will help connect you with others and to nurture and build relationships.

Relationship Building Strategies

These strategies have been proven to be most effective in creating a network of friends and acquaintances. You can do this:

- Join a group with like interests. This is the easiest way to meet people. Involve yourself fully and help out using the skills you most enjoy. I have often volunteered to write the newsletter for a group, an enjoyable role that comes easily. It keeps me connected to other members and I gain a feeling of belonging.

- Don't wait for someone to join a group with you. It may never happen. Be brave and bulge the edges of your comfort zone a little. Look for meet-ups or Google an interest area. Then practise a love language with those you meet.

- Initiate contacts with family and friends. Don't always wait for someone else to make the first move. The most powerful communication is in person, electronic devices next, with writing the least effective. Start where it's most natural for you and then suggest doing something together in person – go for a coffee, lunch, attend an event, take a course, join a group, go on a vacation.

◉ Rekindle friendships from the past that may have lapsed over time. This is the time you may find rewards in looking up your old school or college chums. Attend reunions. Discover where your interests and theirs intersect now. Plan to meet again. How about meeting for coffee or trying a new restaurant for lunch – a new experience for both?

◉ Acknowledge and respond to emails, texts, and tweets of those whose relationships you value.

◉ Follow up and do what you agreed to do. Be true to your word.

◉ Prune the relationships that are no longer in your best interest. Don't be too hasty and risk regrets later. As you build more rewarding relationships, gradually let go of the less rewarding ones.

◉ Join the professional association in your field. Attend conferences and seminars. Volunteer to help or to speak.

◉ Be neighbourly. Volunteer to house or pet sit, water plants, drive a neighbour to an appointment or airport. Attend or organize a group get together with your neighbours.

◉ Involve yourself in your community association, condo board, neighbourhood watch, service club, or faith community.

◉ Join an exercise class, sports or fitness group.

◉ Meet with others to play games of strategy such as crib, bridge, mah-jong, tennis, curling, golf.

◉ Participate in a conversations café.

◉ Expand your role in the lives of children and grandchildren, nieces, nephews, or god children.

◎ Become a mentor, coach, big brother, sister, or volunteer in a school.

◎ Include people of all ages in your life. It's sad when the very old tell me their friends have all passed on. Have young friends, too.

◎ Live in a co-housing or condo complex with others of all ages.

◎ Sign up for a tour or cruise where you can meet others.

◎ Try meeting people on dating sites.

◎ Hang out in a public space with a book in your hand or a dog on its leash. The book or dog could be a conversation starter.

◎ Take a workshop or course where you'll meet people interested in the same subject areas.

◎ Start a group if one with your interests does not already exist.

◎ Listen. Being a good conversationalist does not mean having to do all the talking. Ask an open ended question starting with *what* or *how*. "What projects are intriguing you now?" "How are you doing *today*?" Listen.

◎ Remember the five love languages. If nothing else, practise using more words of affirmation.

A fine balance

Max and Julie, both in their 80's continue to make new friends. Though they live in a rural area apart from other homes, they take a huge interest in others and people flock to their door. Julie and Max ask open ended questions and listen intently with their eyes, smiles, nods, and body language. They share viewpoints and stories. They continue to learn and involve themselves in new adventures, in spite of compromised health. They have a zest for life and are vibrant human beings, traits that immediately attract others of all ages to them. If you're thinking this couple must be highly extraverted, you would be wrong. Time alone is essential to them. Their hobbies are solitary.

It is their passion for people and their compassion for others that trump their introverted tendencies. When they meet a kindred spirit, they become generous with their time and a friendship grows.

Advancing age does not change any of this.

Family

"Family and friends are the perennials in the garden of life."

Lynn Johnston

Families, changed over time and continuing to change, are still the most important social unit in society and the first line of support for most people. The familiar adage that we don't get to choose our family, but do choose our friends is true. If you are currently not close to your family, perhaps now is the time to fertilize those family roots again. Families matter and nurturing those relationships can be worth your time, energy, and attention.

What you can do

- ℗ Acknowledge and celebrate birthdays, anniversaries, and special milestones.

- ℗ Reach out with compassion when a family member faces a challenge or needs care.

- ℗ Be prepared to take on an advocacy role for aging parents. Advocacy is a necessity as parents become frail.

- ℗ Increased elder care requires discussions on important life decisions, potentially bringing family members closer or pushing them further apart. Use active, reflective listening to understand others' positions if they differ from yours. Engage the help of someone skilled in mediation, if necessary, to help you come to mutual understandings and win-win solutions.

◉ Children launched on their own still need you as their compassionate anchor. Use the communication tools they use – a mobile phone, text, photo sharing tools, and social media.

◉ Be compassionate with grandchildren. Some schools are now teaching the love languages to their students. Our 13-year-old granddaughter told us her love language is quality time together. That tells us volumes. It is obvious that our two young adult grandsons love big hugs. And on it goes...

◉ Practise the love languages with family members important to you!

Partner Relationships

"How will I live with my spouse when we're both retired? I'm worried about our relationship."

This concern is often expressed in our Retire to the Life You Design workshops. How will we manage our lives together? When for the past thirty to forty years you've each led your own lives at work or at home, how will you manage this new togetherness? It's like having to start building your relationship all over again. And that is exactly what it takes.

In addition, this new togetherness may occur simultaneously with children leaving the nest and aging parents needing more of your attention. You may actually have four relationship issues to deal with:

1. A loss of work connections

2. A decrease of focus on the daily lives of adult children as they leave the nest

3. The needs of aging parents

4. The expectations you have of yourself and your partner as you journey this new chapter together

All of these can be a major stressor on their own, let alone if they occur at the same time. Separations and divorces are not uncommon. Forewarned and forearmed, many issues can be prevented.

Plan for and expect win-win solutions

In this section we will focus on you and your partner's expectations of your relationship.

Communication is the key

The tools in this book serve as beautiful conversation starters. Set aside a dedicated time to discuss. Don't try this on the fly or when one of you is angry or upset.

Share the values exercise, the introvert/ extravert exercise, and your personality temperament profile. Discuss what each of you needs and wants to be true to yourself. Be careful not to judge and consider one superior to the other. Be considerate of each other's vulnerability, protect each other's self-worth, and keep the door of communication open.

Practise active, reflective listening skills. Focus on genuinely listening for understanding and don't interrupt – use a talking feather like First Nations people if necessary. Use eye contact and respectful body language – avoid degrading grimaces, eye rolls, and exaggerated sighs. Stay seated. Acknowledge what your partner said. Rephrase what you heard to test your understanding. Adjust as needed until you each get it. Then brainstorm options and choose those that make the relationship work for each of you.

Plan for and expect win-win solutions.

Let me share three common real-life scenarios.

Lost independence

When they retired, Gordon and Sarah moved to their dream home in a completely new area. Gordon felt they could save money by managing with one vehicle. They each had hobbies they could truly indulge in their new space. Since they now lived out of town and needed the vehicle to go anywhere, Gordon expected he would drive Sarah where ever she wanted to go. Sarah, who had worked independently as a nurse with her own vehicle up to then, lamented, "Because Gordon wants to go everywhere I go, I've lost my independence. I'm aware he's in the car waiting for me and I feel I need to hurry and finish what I'm doing." The issue was resolved when Sarah discussed her frustration and the two of them came to a new agreement. They involved themselves more in the community, each with some of their own activities as well as some together activities, driving themselves to their individual involvements. The need for Gordon to go everywhere together decreased and Sarah regained the independence she wanted.

Role shifting

Raj and Naheen had well established tasks each was responsible for in managing their household. When they retired, the balance was no longer so even. Naheen felt she was carrying most of the load and Raj was slacking off. Raj and Naheen sat down to discuss all the household tasks that needed doing (see the Interests, Skills, and Activities Sampler in Appendix C for a start of such a list). They then negotiated a new division of labour that worked for both, including switching some roles and taking turns on others. Raj found he enjoyed cooking and trying his hand at baking artisan breads. Naheen enjoyed being in charge of kitchen cleanup and doing the household accounts. They shared the laundry, house cleaning, and garbage removal, with a new awareness of what needed to be done around the house.

> **Working together**
>
> *I had been working for years part time in my home-based business when we relocated to a new city and Tom started his own home-based business. Initially Tom felt we could easily share a desk and computer in one office. I was skeptical, but in the interest of a new togetherness, was willing to try it for a month or two. After the trial period, we agreed that we really did need our own offices and Tom converted a spare bedroom for this purpose. By being willing to try a new arrangement for a period and recognizing when something was not working as expected, conflict was avoided. We still share the printer.*

The key in these examples is communicating your own needs while understanding and appreciating the other person's needs; to discuss and negotiate a shared agreement; to be willing to try something different when something is not working as well as expected.

Tips for Healthy Couple Relationships

In addition to these examples, here are a few more tips proven to help you navigate the new together territory.

For each of you:

- ⊚ Do some things together and some things apart.

- ⊚ Share common interests. Share some of the stories of your apart experiences with each other.

- ⊚ Have your own individual friends as well as couple friends.

- ⊚ Create a space in your home that is strictly your own. An arts or crafts space?

The key in these examples is communicating your own needs.

A workshop? A man cave? This space is strictly hands off for your partner. You can leave it as messy as you like without comments or 'helpful' re-arrangements by partners.

As a couple:

- Plan a regular date night for just the two of you, just like you did when you were starting your relationship. How does dinner and a movie sound? A Friday night leisurely nibbling your favourite finger foods while sipping a glass of wine and talking?

- Plan a weekly outing as a surprise for the other. Take turns doing this.

- Be a tourist in your own neighbourhood or city. See all the sites tourists come to see.

- Set a goal to walk or cycle all the trails in your community or one nearby.

- Take up one new hobby or join a group together.

- Do a volunteer activity together.

- Do a fitness activity together.

- Read the same book and discuss it together.

- Watch a movie and discuss it together.

- Buy season's tickets to an arts performance.

- Host a dinner that you share with friends – share the planning and execution.

- Celebrate each other's birthdays, anniversaries, and milestones.

Remember to use the love languages.

Choose to feed the Good Wolf with kindness, love and compassion.

Choose to feed the Good Wolf with kindness, love, and compassion. Your relationships will be strong and new ones will sprout.

"Kindness is the language which the deaf can hear and the blind can see."

Mark Twain

Society

"Be the change you wish to see in the world."

Mahatma Gandhi

Being kind to yourself, choosing to feed the Good Wolf, and using the five love languages are all ways of being the change you wish to see in the world. Because, as Fred Rogers says, "There is something of yourself that you leave at every meeting with another person."

Intentionally furthering this compassion to society as a whole is an additional way. By embracing a cause you care about, you can make a meaningful difference to your own community and perhaps even the globe. You can live your life with a purpose beyond your own immediate circle.

Something is missing

My email inbox contained this message from Gary.

'Where were you when I retired? Since I retired I have learned to sail and play a musical instrument. I have taken up art. I spend winters in the south playing golf. I'm involved with my grandchildren. I seemingly have a perfect life, and yet... something is missing. I just wanted to say congratulations on what you're doing. It's too late for me now.'

Gary wasn't asking for my help although I did write him back. One thing I told him – it's never too late!

Gary had enjoyed a traditional retirement for a time. But without having a purpose, something to care about and contribute to that's greater than himself, this lifestyle can get stale and boring. Six to eighteen months in, when the vacation feel wears off, your initial goals are met, the dream trip has been completed, and the house has been renovated, what's next? What will you do with your gift of longevity then?

Without contributing in some small or larger way to a societal cause something is missing.

Without contributing in some small or larger way to a societal cause something is missing.

The needs of society are many. There are so many causes to be compassionate about. Every fundraising campaign points them out to us, especially at Christmas. Where and how can you begin to sort through the options?

1. Begin by choosing to be FOR something rather than AGAINST something. Instead of being AGAINST war, for instance, be FOR peace. Not AGAINST disease, but FOR health. Not hate, but love. Not scarcity, but abundance (e.g., food, clothing, shelter). Choose to live in a positive space.

2. Next consider what societal cause you are FOR. What do you care most about? What are you passionate about? What stories in the news move you to tears or to action?

3. In the following exercise, place a check mark beside any of the 40+ causes you most care about.

If this is difficult, ask yourself if you care most about people's basic needs such as food, shelter, clothing, safety or security, or the higher level needs of love, belonging, self-esteem, and self-fulfilment.

What You Most Care About

☐	Abundance	☐	Energy
☐	Aesthetics	☐	Environment
☐	Art	☐	Equality
☐	Authenticity	☐	Ethics
☐	Awareness	☐	Fairness
☐	Beauty	☐	Family
☐	Civility	☐	Finance
☐	Communication	☐	Fitness
☐	Community	☐	Freedom
☐	Compassion	☐	Generosity
☐	Connection	☐	Growth
☐	Conservation	☐	Harmony
☐	Curiosity	☐	Healing
☐	Democracy	☐	Health
☐	Design	☐	History
☐	Dignity	☐	Honour
☐	Economy	☐	Human Potential
☐	Education	☐	Human Rights
☐	Empowerment	☐	Humour

☐ Innovation	☐ Protection
☐ Joy	☐ Quality
☐ Justice	☐ Relationships
☐ Knowledge	☐ Respect
☐ Language	☐ Safety
☐ Literacy	☐ Science
☐ Love	☐ Security
☐ Mathematics	☐ Self-Esteem
☐ Moderation	☐ Self-Actualization
☐ Morality	☐ Serenity
☐ Music	☐ Simplicity
☐ Nature	☐ Space
☐ Nutrition	☐ Spirit
☐ Opinion	☐ Systems
☐ Opportunity	☐ Technology
☐ Peace	☐ Theatre
☐ Policy	☐ Tranquility
☐ Politics	☐ Transportation
☐ Positive Living	☐ Trust
☐ Preservation	☐ Trends
☐ Principles	☐ Understanding

- ☐ Unity

- ☐ Usefulness

- ☐ Vitality

- ☐ Wisdom

- ☐ Zest

- ☐ Something else...

The following are four examples of what others care about and what they are doing about it.

> ## Joy, freedom, simplicity, compassion, family
>
> *John owned a medium sized high tech company. At 50-something he wanted off the corporate train that was becoming more and more stressful to him, threatening burn out. But how to get off that fast moving train? John sold the business and tried consulting for a number of years. Tired of travel, John knew he really just wanted the freedom and simplicity of being home in his large house and garden but with something meaningful to do that makes a difference to society. He and his wife Betty, an early childhood educator, had raised five children in the home that was now an almost-empty nest. John and Betty decided to foster children. This was a perfect fit for both and has brought much joy and meaning to their lives. Over the years, they have given as many as thirty 4 to 8-year-olds (their preferred age group) a new beginning with foster parents who love to nurture, teach, cook, drive, garden, camp, and provide all the opportunities a stable loving family gives their offspring.*

Literacy, self-esteem, empowerment

After Evelyn retired from a multi-track work history, her love of reading made her consider the plight of children and adults who could not enjoy what she valued so much. Evelyn was particularly concerned about adults who stumbled through life hiding their reading deficiency. She chose to volunteer for a not-for-profit literacy organization that partners children and adults with volunteers who help them learn and practise reading comprehension. Helping adults learn to read has made a huge difference to them, increasing self-esteem and empowering each to function more confidently in society.

Music, opportunity, positive living

Duncan and Ann love music, particularly choral music. When a group in their community started a singing group for at-risk youth, they jumped in with both feet, becoming singing buddies, coaches, and mentors to the youth. The young people choose the music they all sing, including rap music, something totally new to this retired couple. The opportunity to connect with at-risk youth on their turf with their music has opened doors to other opportunities to mentor them into choosing positive living options.

Health, fitness, healing

Mario had been my go-to computer guru for years. Over those years, I learned there was much more to him than his amazing abilities to fix my computer. It started when a very fit Mario arrived at my office after months of sessions at the gym. That fitness interest evolved into Mario doing and teaching qigong. Approaching 60, Mario gradually phased out of computer technology and into opening his own business teaching qigong – the practice of breathing, gentle movement, and visualization. He offers his studio for use by other healing health practitioners and for pay-what-you-can group meditation sessions. Providing opportunities to adopt good health and fitness practices has become Mario's cause and passion in the second half of his life.

Considering the causes you checked for yourself, can you identify one, two, or more that you would like to support with your time, your talents, or your money? Circle those causes.

Next, can you identify a specific issue represented by the causes you circled? Furthermore, can you identify the individuals or groups that you feel most passionate about?

Here are examples of how you can put this together:

WHAT I CARE ABOUT	SPECIFIC ISSUE I CARE ABOUT	WHO FOR
e.g., Abundance	breakfast and lunches	kids in school
	affordable housing	all families
	sustainable agriculture	third world communities
	jobs	people with disabilities
Environment	reducing CO2 emissions	my industry
	preserving urban forests	my city

Now it's your turn. Start with the cause and then think about the specifics.

WHAT I CARE ABOUT	SPECIFIC ISSUE I CARE ABOUT	WHO FOR

Write a draft sentence or two that spells out what you want to live your life FOR – to be the change you wish to see in the world at home, in your community, or in society. I want to live FOR

In *Appendix A* or your journal, record how you want to be compassionate.

> **Passionate about human potential**
>
> *I am most passionate about Human Potential and Usefulness. When I meet people 'stuck' on how to find the work or fulfilment they want, I want to jump in to offer help. Don't know how to plan a fulfilling career? Let me guide you through a proven planning process. Stuck not knowing your passion or purpose? Scared about retirement? Bored when retired? Let me show you ways to become revitalized. It hurts to see people struggle, give up, and watch potential go to waste. Let's put human potential to use!*

Imagine, sang John Lennon. Imagine if each one of us made one commitment, set one intention, took one small action that made society a better place. That's all it would take to effect change in society.

Tsunamis, earthquakes, floods, 9/11, disasters of any kind bring out the best in people. People flock to help or donate money. Perspectives change. Compassion grows and multiplies.

Act on what you're passionate about without a disaster pushing you to action.

Let's continue to be useful! Imagine what would happen if we did!

Discover how in the next chapter.

Long life + long health = long usefulness

CHAPTER 6

BE A CONTRIBUTOR

"We make a living by what we get. We make a life by what we give."

Winston Churchill

You are already a contributor. Through working, volunteering, or being who you are, you are contributing to society in some way, knowingly or unknowingly. Gary contributes to his own wellness by being creative, active, and fit, and to his family by spending time with his grandchildren. The missing part may be contributing to something more, a societal cause he cares about. Being a contributor is about focusing not only on 'me' but also on 'we'.

Being a Contributor is what we are *Being Well* for!

When current work ends, there is a new opportunity to contribute and in the process, create a new purpose for our lives.

For increasing numbers of us, this means continuing to work in some way. Gary Burtless of the Brookings Institution calculates that in America 50% of men and 40% of women with a bachelor's degree are now in the workforce between ages 62-74. The numbers are smaller for those with a high school education but still significant and growing at 32% and 25%. As education increases, so do the percentages, with 65% of men and 50% of women holding a professional or a doctorate degree remaining in the workforce between ages 62-74. In Europe, the numbers are smaller but equally striking.

The Canadian Sun Life Financial Unretirement™ Index 2014 reports that 27% of those surveyed (3, 005 working Canadians from age 30-65) expect to work full time at age 66 with 28% expecting to be fully retired and not working. Expectations may change, but based on a similar trend in all rich countries, it is not surprising that as many as 72% expect to be working full or part time at age 66 because they need or want to work.

Being a contributor is about focusing
not only on 'me'
but also on 'we'.

Need to Work

Money problem

Ann, 68, a former colleague, confided that she would never be able to retire. She had taken long breaks from work in her 40s to enjoy a care-free lifestyle. Ann had spent her money and was now in a situation that required a regular work income to meet her most basic needs. We discussed options for living in a more affordable community close to her son and his family, in combination with a work option she could continue for a long time and that would fulfil her needs for regular people interaction. Ann was close to making the change when instead, she had to refocus on healing from a life-threatening illness that she unfortunately did not survive.

If, like Ann, you're concerned about having your money last as long as your life, consult a professional financial advisor to guide you through your financial options. Consult a career advisor/ coach/ retirement professional to guide you through alternate work options. You may be surprised to find that you won't need to work quite as long or as hard as you had thought. Or that you discover work options that you will love for many years that won't feel like work. You won't know for sure until you crunch the numbers and check out all your options.

Finding enough

Christine, 70, Authentic Blue, participated in a career planning workshop I facilitated. Christine was exhausted from working as a personal care giver in four jobs. She loved her work and was attending the workshop to replace one of the jobs that had ended. Like Ann, Christine needed to continue to work and was dependent on the income to pay her mortgage. In private, I probed her income needs and learned that she did not expect to pay off her mortgage within her lifetime. I was able to point her to resources and options that could relieve her of some of her financial burden so she would not have to work quite as hard as before.

These are not isolated stories. Indications are that women, in particular, are vulnerable to poverty as they age.

Both Ann and Christine had meaningful work but needed to find new ways to live and work that could sustain them through life's next chapter. Work is not a four letter word. Okay, it IS a four letter word AND it can be rewarding and packaged in a multitude of ways to meet many of your needs. As Gary Burtless found, baby boomers are continuing to work. Increasingly they do so on their own terms. Read on for more...

Want to Work

"Work is an opportunity for discovering and shaping the place where the self meets the world."

David Whyte

With increasing longevity, baby boomers (Statistics Canada reports are those born between 1946-1964) and older folks can continue to contribute to society by

- continuing to be productive

- using cognitive and creative skills that do not decline as do physical skills

- sharing their individual and collective wisdom that increases as we age

The Canadian Association of Retired Persons calls these individuals 'zoomers' – boomers with zip!

Why Contribute?

We contribute because we all have the same needs for physical comfort, security, love, self-esteem, and self-actualization (self-fulfilment), as Abraham H. Maslow shows in his Hierarchy of Needs pyramid.

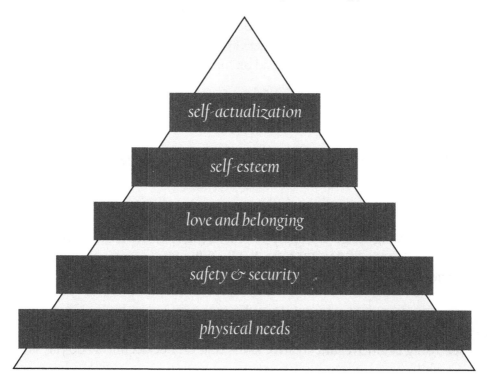

At the base of the hierarchy are physical needs that drive us to continue to work to be able to afford food, shelter, and clothing. Safety and security needs drive us to work for personal and financial security and a safety net against accidents and illness. Love and belonging needs drive us to work because of the need to belong to a group, a company, or a profession, connecting us to colleagues and mentors. Self-esteem needs are met through feeling useful and necessary in the world, as Maslow himself says:

"Satisfaction of the self-esteem need leads to feelings of self-confidence, worth, strength, capability, and adequacy, of being useful and necessary in the world.

Even if all these needs are satisfied, we may still often (if not always) expect that a new discontent and restlessness will soon develop, unless the individual is doing what he is fitted for. A musician must make music, an artist must paint, a poet must write, if he is to be ultimately happy. What a man can be, he must be. This need we may call self-actualization."

 ## Why Work Tool

Paid or volunteer work, casual or more formal, full or part time are a means of fulfilling our basic and higher level needs on the hierarchy.

Check all the needs your work currently provides. Then complete the chart that follows.

Physical needs

    ☐   Money for food, shelter, and clothing – survival needs

Safety and security needs

    ☐   Money for health care, supplements, and pharmaceuticals

    ☐   Health care benefits

    ☐   Pension benefits

    ☐   Travel insurance benefits

    ☐   Savings for a rainy day

    ☐   Savings for aids to daily living when frail, ill, or dependent

    ☐   Stability of a regular routine

Love and belonging needs

- ☐ Affiliation – being an integral part of a family, a group, a community, an organization, a company, an industry, a profession

- ☐ Feeling connected with coworkers, clients, or customers

- ☐ Mattering to someone or something – feeling significant in another's life

- ☐ Being an active participant in society – filling a need in my tribe or society

- ☐ Being spiritually connected to a higher power

Self-esteem needs

- ☐ Identity

- ☐ Recognition

- ☐ Status

- ☐ Power

- ☐ Knowledge

- ☐ Competence

- ☐ Leadership

- ☐ Problem solving

- ☐ Creativity

- ☐ Productivity

- ☐ Service

- ☐ Usefulness

☐ Intellectual stimulation

☐ Success

☐ Wealth

Self-actualization needs

☐ Meaning – knowing who I am

☐ Living authentically – being true to who I am

☐ Freedom – to be and do

☐ Purpose – knowing why I am here and living it

☐ Passion – being engaged in what I care about

☐ Joy – the awareness of being in the present moment

Refer also to the values important to you from *Chapter 2: Be Who You Are* for needs specific to the four personality temperaments.

When you leave current work, you need replacement activities to fulfill the needs that were met by work. Replacement activities can include working at something different or in a different way, taking on a volunteer role or a project, learning a new skill or knowledge, and joyful leisure activities.

What do you need?

When she retired from a rewarding teaching career, Connie did a quiz in which she identified the needs that her work fulfilled and then identified what she thought her future needs would be. From this exercise she learned that needs don't change in retirement. They are just met in different ways.

Connie's work satisfied needs of affiliation with a group, leadership, recognition, intellect, problem solving, and security. In retirement she found different groups and organizations in which she could volunteer, help others, take leadership roles, and meet these same needs. But she also had more time to focus on needs that were at the bottom of her list such as freedom, adventure, aesthetics and spiritual needs. Her priorities changed in retirement as she became aware of all the wonderful opportunities that were available to her. They continue to change as she chooses what brings her the most joy.

Some of the wonderful opportunities Connie found were organizing a group of former colleagues that meets weekly to play mah-jong, a game she has taught them; taking charge of donations for the toy and children's books room at her church's giant garage sale; travelling to a needy country to take essential supplies to families; hosting a group of youth in an exchange program; and being part of and coordinating a seniors' group that's learning art and calligraphy.

Connie meets her evolving aesthetic and spiritual needs by learning to paint and by studying and deepening her awareness and understanding of spirituality.

Identifying Current and Future Needs

Use the Why Work tool to help identify your personal needs and what you need to replace when you stop working.

My needs satisfied by current work	My needs when I leave current work
e.g., identity, income, people connections, contribution	e.g., identity, people connections, freedom, joy, belonging, sense of purpose, a reason to get up in the morning, a reason to get out of the house

My needs satisfied by current work	My needs when I leave current work

Your task is to replace what you need from the work you leave with other activities that satisfy those needs.

If you need income security, a safety net for unforeseen circumstances, or wealth creation, consult a professional financial advisor. There are options beside paid work that could satisfy these needs and these advisors are the experts that can help you.

For hundreds of ideas on possible joyful leisure activities, refer to the Interests, Skills and Activities Sampler in *Appendix B* and the Sample Activities for your colour in *Appendix C*. Highlight those activities that you would like to continue or start doing.

Meeting needs – 5 examples

Walter

When my older brother left his position as leader in a large corporation in his later 50s, he filled his needs for authenticity, freedom, independence, identity, recognition, status, competence, intellectual stimulation, leadership, and problem solving by starting a consulting company and doing contract work where his knowledge and expertise were valued. He was invited to join a corporate board that met additional needs for affiliation and travel and health benefits.

Heather

When athletic Heather retired from an administrative public service position, she threw herself into the outdoor pursuits she loved by joining an outdoors club. She skis in the winter and hikes in the summer with this group and goes on longer trips with them, too. Heather is also an active volunteer in her church community where she contributes her ideas and skills. Her affiliation, freedom, contributing, and adventure needs are met living in this authentic way.

Al

When Al, a school principal, retired, he joined an international service club. The club required regular attendance and active participation in all its philanthropic projects that filled his needs for affiliation, contributing, leadership, and intellectual stimulation.

Colleen

Colleen retired from a retail position in a home décor store. Her first love is weaving. Being a member of two weaving guilds meets her needs for affiliation, creativity, mental stimulation, and contributing. Through the guild she attends training workshops and contributes some of her creations to help fund community projects.

Patricia

Patricia, a specialist in business modelling who retired once, was soon recruited to work on a complex project. During the year or so she was not doing paid work, she volunteered as the president of the choral association of which she was a member, bringing new energy , skills, and enthusiasm to the role. This interim role was one of several that met her needs for leadership, affiliation, intellectual stimulation, creativity, and contributing.

You may have noticed that the common theme in these examples is contributing through paid or volunteer work roles. This results in being a part of something bigger than yourself, and one of the ways of filling the need for affiliation.

The possibilities for a range of work options are numerous. Gradually reducing your work hours or finding a new way to work are possibilities for you, too, to consider.

How to Work – Paid Work Options

If you want or need to work for money, you have many options beyond full time work with regular hours. The 9-5 Monday to Friday routine that was the norm in the 50s and 60s has become rare in our global, information–based economy.

How to work with monetary rewards include:

- Continue to work as you do now – no need for change

- Phase into a shorter work week – work 2-3-4 days instead of 5 – a growing trend

- Work 1, 2, or 3 weeks out of 4 each month

- Work seasonally – spring, fall, winter or summer or a combination

- Work flex hours – go into work later or leave earlier; work longer days with a day off each week

- Job share – share one position with another person

- Work only mornings or only afternoons

- Work full or part time at a new job in the same field or industry

- Choose a new career direction

- Work from home – some of the time

- Work from home – most of the time

- Virtual work – from anywhere in the world

- Self-employment – a solo enterprise

- Project work – a body of work with a beginning and end

- Contract – project or continuing contract work

- Consulting – project or continuing consulting work – in your field of expertise

- Locum work – spell off other professionals on vacation

- Casual work

- On-call work

- Temporary work

- Shift work

- Entrepreneur – operate a business that employs others

- ⊘ Start a new business

- ⊘ Buy an existing business

- ⊘ Buy a franchise

- ⊘ Own/ Operate a virtual franchise – or a direct marketing business – promote a product or service you believe in

- ⊘ Talent pool with other professionals

- ⊘ Multi-track – combine a number of paid work options

How to Work – Volunteer Work Options

Work is not only what you do to make money. Work is also volunteer work, housework, home maintenance, parenting and caregiving work, philanthropy projects, or anything you choose to contribute your time or talents to.

How to work without monetary rewards include:

- ⊘ Pro bono work – contribute your talents and waive or donate your usual fees to charity.

- ⊘ Casual – helping family members, neighbours, or friends as needed when you are available.

- ⊘ Random – surprise someone with a random act of kindness.

- ⊘ Occasional – e.g., during a disaster or a crisis event, a fundraising event, or during an election

- ⊘ Participate actively yourself in a fundraising event such as running a marathon or riding in a bike-athon.

- ⊘ Donation – create something on your own or with others to donate to a cause you care about.

◎ On call – work only during a specific shift or time frame as needed.

◎ Flexible hours.

◎ Seasonal – volunteer only during a season that you are available.

◎ From home – on your own terms, such as repair bikes or computers to donate to needy families.

◎ With your partner, family members, or friends – choose a cause you want to collectively contribute to, such as making meals for a homeless shelter, building or renovating a home for someone.

◎ Ad hoc working group or committee – that disbands when the project is completed.

◎ Project volunteer – take on a project you enjoy that you can do when it suits you, such as newsletter editor, archivist, website design or maintenance, data base administrator.

◎ Formal volunteer – commit to a regular time and day when you work a shift for an organization.

◎ Formal volunteer – an executive or committee member of a working group, committee or board of directors.

◎ Contract volunteer – such as teach English as a second language at home or abroad.

◎ Multi-track – combine a number of volunteer work options.

Go online to discover volunteer opportunities and organizations to join the millions who are already contributing on their own terms, in their own way, doing what they care about. You will find links to get you started in *References and Resources* section at the back of this book.

In my 70s, I work in this multi-track way:

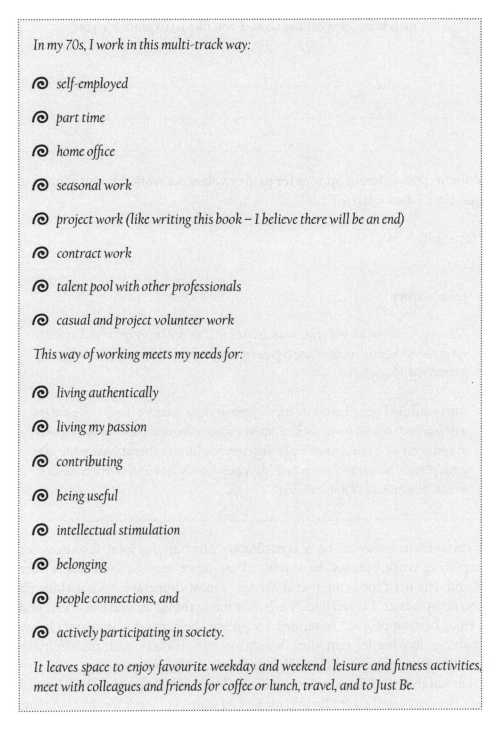

- *self-employed*

- *part time*

- *home office*

- *seasonal work*

- *project work (like writing this book – I believe there will be an end)*

- *contract work*

- *talent pool with other professionals*

- *casual and project volunteer work*

This way of working meets my needs for:

- *living authentically*

- *living my passion*

- *contributing*

- *being useful*

- *intellectual stimulation*

- *belonging*

- *people connections, and*

- *actively participating in society.*

It leaves space to enjoy favourite weekday and weekend leisure and fitness activities, meet with colleagues and friends for coffee or lunch, travel, and to Just Be.

Which ways of working would you like to explore for you?

....

....

....

Knowing the different options for paid or volunteer work, I know your next question: *What exactly will I do?*

Have Skills – Will Work

John's story

The trim, straight-backed gentleman dressed in a snappy navy crew-neck sweater sat at the back of the room taking copious notes at a public library talk I was giving. I wondered who he was.

Afterwards, he lingered to ask if I knew of any work for someone like him. He and his wife had both retired from teaching careers. Post retirement they worked together in a business for a time. Now his wife was content with activities at home while John could think of no options for someone like him in his 70s. "I'm being a jerk around the house," he admitted. "I feel so useless".

John needed a way to be a contributor. After giving John resources for exploring work options, he contacted me again months later, no further ahead. His need for being useful became almost desperate. "What skills do you enjoy using?" I asked him. "I'm handy fixing things around the house, and I enjoy helping people," he replied. I suggested he contact a company I knew that was looking for part-time, handy, mature workers with the ability to communicate professionally with homeowners. The company was willing to train suitable candidates in the specific skills needed for the job. John followed up. His next email excitedly told me he had started to work for the company.

John's story shows that we:

- Have transferable skills we can draw on.

- Can learn new specific skills.

- May find a rewarding career/ life if we are open to trying something new or different. It's not too late.

Yes, you can still work even if you don't need the money. And if you do need money, paid work is one solution.

Career/ Life Focus

The world of work consists of four main areas: working with data, people, things, ideas, or a combination thereof.

 Rank your career/ life focus 1, 2, 3, 4 in the order that is true for you.

I enjoy working with:

- ☐ Data – facts and information, numbers and money

- ☐ People – serving, advising, healing, coordinating, leading

- ☐ Things – physical objects, tools and equipment

- ☐ Ideas – thinking, reasoning, analyzing, creating, innovating

Career/ life focus correlates with your personality temperament. The underline means it's your dominant focus, with the others auxiliary to it.

Inquiring Greens focus on <u>IDEAS</u>, DATA, PEOPLE

Organized Golds focus on <u>DATA</u>, PEOPLE

Authentic Blues focus on <u>PEOPLE</u>, IDEAS

Resourceful Oranges focus on <u>THINGS</u>, PEOPLE

My family is a great source of inspiration for me because in the second half of life they chose careers using natural strengths focused on data, people, things, or ideas, or a combination of the four.

Data and people

My father set a perfect example as he continued to work into his 80s. As an accountant, he focused on helping those without the skills to complete their income tax returns, continuing until his eye sight failed. His career focus as an Organized Gold was data and people. He served on community boards and committees all his life.

People

Like other women of her generation, my mother devoted her life to raising her family. With compassion for others, she became a friendly visitor to those who were isolated from their own families. She volunteered in her church at bake sales and other fundraisers and was an active member of several church groups.

Data, people, and ideas

My younger brother, Frank, is also an Organized Gold whose first career was in banking, a data and people industry. In the second half of life he focuses on data, people, and ideas. An entrepreneur and natural leader, he shifted from banking to consulting for not-for-profit organizations. He facilitates workshops on board governance and business planning, building on both his business experience and his experience as a volunteer board member of a number of service organizations.

Ideas, data, things

My Authentic Blue/ Organized Gold sister Joanne (people, ideas, data), a seniors advocate and leader, and my Inquiring Green/ Resourceful Orange older brother Walter (ideas, data, things) are mentioned elsewhere in this book. Look for them on pages 100 and 123. After leaving his consulting career, my older brother has returned to his first love of things by designing and building fine furniture for his home.

Career/ Life Focus Skills

With significant life experience under your belt, you already have a huge body of skills at your disposal to put to use. It would be a waste to park them on a shelf now, shut the door, and forget you have them. They are a part of you already.

What matters is identifying those skills you have that you now want to use. Skills are competencies that fall into two main categories:

- specific to a career/ life focus or a specific role

- transferable among any number of roles

Specific Skills generally require education or workplace training. Examples are medical skills, transport driving skills, technology skills, business skills. Use your specific skills to keep working in the same role or field you are competent in. Or learn a new specific skill to change directions – see *Chapter 7: Be Curious.*

Your specific skills:

....

....

....

Transferable Skills are portable among different areas and stages of your life and from one role to another. They come from experience of any kind, at home, at school, at work, and in the community. Examples are communication skills, computer skills, and teamwork skills. Use your transferable skills to branch out to other fields of work or to work in a different way.

Transferable Skills Tool

 Circle all the skills you have that you enjoy using now or may use in the future. Star the skills you would like to learn or develop further. Ignore the ones you don't have, don't enjoy using, and don't want to learn.

Universal Fundamental Skills

Reading, writing, listening, speaking, numerical reasoning, teamwork, creative thinking, critical thinking, problem solving, computer literacy – keyboarding, word processing.

Data Skills – facts and information, numbers and money

Measuring, counting, estimating, categorizing, calculating, budgeting, observing, monitoring, testing, record keeping, scheduling, organizing, planning, logistical skills, sequential thinking skills (noticing a natural order).

People Skills – serving, advising, coordinating, leading, healing, nuturing

Facilitating, teaching, training, coaching, counselling, advising, advocating, mentoring, empathizing, mediating, negotiating, coordinating, leading, supervising, managing, recruiting, selling, influencing, integrative thinking skills (noticing similarities).

Things Skills – physical objects, tools and equipment

Operating, maintaining, repairing, troubleshooting, constructing, producing, building, renovating, installing, restoring, improvising, adapting, implementing, performing, physical skills, hands-on skills, contextual thinking skills (noticing the present context).

Ideas Skills – thinking, reasoning, creating, innovating

Analyzing, strategizing, reasoning, visualizing, theorizing, innovating, inventing, mobilizing, planning, developing, creating, designing, initiating, explaining, interpreting, critiquing, differential thinking skills (noticing differences).

Skills, Interests and Activities Sampler

I hope you have come to know you have a variety of skills to use as you wish – plus new ones you can learn.

Go to *Appendix C* and *Appendix D* for an extensive list of activity ideas where you can use your skills for enjoyable future work or enjoyable leisure activities.

Idea Generator #1

After identifying potential current and future activities in The Sampler, complete this easy tool that combines interests and skills to spark potential activities. With their permission, I borrowed this tool from a book co-authored by my publisher, Jo, and by my daughter, Colleen: *A Career In Your Suitcase, A Practical Guide to Creating Meaningful Work Anywhere – 4th Edition.*

Across the top horizontal row, write 5 things you love – in noun form.

Along the left vertical column, write 5 things you are good at – in verb form ending in 'ing'.

In each square, combine what you love with each of the five skills to spark 25 ideas for you to consider, even if these combinations seem strange for now.

Here is a fictional example of interests and skills often mentioned by people in my workshops.

I love ⟶ I am good at ↓	grand-children	gardens	golf	travel	home decor
organizing	organizing grand-children	organizing gardens	organizing golf	organizing travel	organizing home decor
planning	planning grand-children	planning gardens	planning golf	planning travel	planning home decor
designing	designing grand-children	designing gardens	designing golf	designing travel	designing home decor
nurturing	nurturing grand-children	nurturing gardens	nurturing golf	nurturing travel	nurturing home decor
computer research	researching grand-children	researching gardens	researching golf	researching travel	researching home decor

Some of these combinations are downright laughable, like designing grandchildren. This could, however, lead one to thinking about designing and organizing outdoor activities for grandchildren, possibly combining gardening, golf, travel, and grandchildren. Combining several of your interests and skills could also lead to something like travel advisor, greenhouse worker, floral designer, event planner, home organizer, interior designer, or home stager.

I love ⟶					
I am good at ↓					

You now have 25 ideas. Even though the combinations may sound odd, you are looking for one or more that could be intriguing. Express these in a way and in words that make sense to you.

....

....

....

There's much more...

If you feel something is still missing, that could be because we have not yet identified how you can contribute to the causes you identified in *Chapter 5: Be Compassionate.*

That's where we're going next.

Natural Talents/ Roles

Natural talents include strengths identified in *Chapter 5: Be Compassionate* pages and skills identified in *Chapter 6: Be a Contributor* pages.

Talents can also be natural roles that are inherent in your colour temperament. Linda Berens, who created the original work on which Personality Dimensions and the Retirement Dimensions tool was built, suggests roles that come most naturally to each of the four temperaments.

Berens also suggests that temperament's core needs are closely linked to the Self-esteem and Self-actualization needs of Maslow's Hierarchy.

Instead of a colour, Berens uses a natural role for each temperament name. I've combined the Retirement Dimensions' colour name, with Berens' natural role name, and a career/ life focus as a guide to how you might contribute. I've also added the core needs Berens identifies for each temperament.

In the personality temperaments most like you, a lot like you, perhaps somewhat like you, and even least like you, underline the talents and roles that interest you.

Authentic Blue Temperament – Catalyst Role – People and Ideas Focus

Berens' core needs* – meaning, significance; identity
Natural Talents and Roles:

Catalyst – bring out the best in others

Mentor/ Foreseer – help develop the potential of others

Advocate/ Interpreter – explain information to others; speak on behalf of a person or cause

Harmonizer/ Mediator – seek to establish harmony between individuals and groups

Champion – inspire the potential in others, champion a cause

Counsellor – know what to say to help others; know the deeper motivation of others

Facilitator/ Diplomat – ease relationships and build bridges between people and ideas

Transformer – bring individuals and organizations to a higher level of functioning

Inquiring Green Temperament – Theorist Role – Ideas, Data, and People Focus

Berens' core needs – mastery and self-control, knowledge and competence
Natural Talents and Roles:

Theorist – seek objective, universal truths

Visionary – think of future realities and implications

Strategist – think of all possible contingencies

Mobilizer/ Director – find talented people to accomplish strategic goals

Marshall – lead or guide people to get a job done

Engineer/ Inventor – design systems

Categorize – create categories to differentiated data and information

Analyst – reason based on objective facts and information

Organized Gold Temperament – Stabilizer Role – Data and People Focus

Berens' core needs – membership and contributing; responsibility and duty
Natural Talents and Roles:

Stabilizer/ Traditionalist – stabilize with a focus on traditional ways of doing things

Supervisor/ Inspector – regulate and standardize for consistency of quality
Supporter – support organizations with talents or financial aid

Rule Maker/ Enforcer – stabilize organizations and facilitate accountability

Logistician – ensure the right things and information get to the right people at the right time

Monitor – ensure things are done right

Provider/ Caretaker – provide for the comfort and well-being of others
Protector – preserve what is needed or wanted in the world

Resourceful Orange Temperament – Improviser Role – Things and People Focus

Berens' core needs – freedom to act now; need to make an impact
Natural Talents and Roles:

Improviser/ Negotiator – vary response to what is going on in the moment with an acute reading of nonverbal cues

Operator – operate machinery or systems; persuade

Executor – ensure things happen

Producer – produce products and motivate people to action

Presenter/ Performer – inform others and get things done with impact

Crisis Manager – respond and adapt to the needs of the moment

Tactician – skillful management for a desired result

Troubleshooter – assess an object or situation and find a solution

*BERENS' CORE NEEDS – Adapted with permission from Linda Berens' descriptions of the Four Temperaments, now called Essential Motivators.

Important Points

1. Do not restrict yourself to only the roles in one temperament. Remember you are a blend of several temperaments. Do use your natural talents and roles as a guide to potential self-esteem and self-fulfilment.

2. As you get older and wiser, the Catalyst roles leading to self-actualization may start to appeal to you more, as they have for others in this life stage.

A wise elder

Judy retired from a career as a math teacher. Being spiritually enlightened, she was drawn to positive aging and the role of the wise elder described in Reb Zalman's book, From Age-ing to Sage-ing, A Profound New Vision of Growing Older. *A wise elder is a person who has or develops a talent for the Catalyst Role, for bringing out the best in themselves and others. Judy has a passion for movies, seemingly knowing them all. As her first initiative, she combined her two interests of movies and wise eldering to create a popular workshop using movies as a thinking and discussion tool for ageing well and living a fulfilling life. Now with 67 years of life experience, Judy has expanded the work she started by creating new workshops, becoming a Soulcollage® facilitator, and speaking at seminars and conferences, contributing to society in the way she is inspired to do.*

Such inspiration comes from lingering in the *Just Be* circle and wandering in the *Be Curious* circle for a while. Try it for yourself and don't be surprised at what ideas emerge that inspire you.

The wise elder role can be expressed in many ways.

Maggie Kuhn, founder of the Grey Panthers and quoted in Reb Zalman's book, suggests these are the five key roles needed in society for which those of us in our second half or third age are particularly talented. I call them the Five M's.

 ๏ Mentors – who share their wisdom and teach others

- Mediators–who resolve family, community, civil, and intergenerational conflicts

- Monitors – who serve as watchdogs of public bodies in the community, the nation, or the world

- Mobilizers – who marshal ideas and people to effect social change

- Motivators – who urge people towards public good

Does one of these put a fire in your belly?

 Idea Generator #2

Use the same directions as Idea Generator #1. This time, write what you care most about (from *Chapter 5: Be Compassionate*) in the top horizontal row and the natural roles you love (from Berens' personality temperaments above) in the vertical column. Then combine the two in each square for 25 ideas.

My own example looks like this.

I care about ⟶	human potential – aging polulation	family	nature	literacy	beauty
natural talents/roles ↓	facilitating human potential	facilitating family	facilitating nature	facilitating literacy	facilitating beauty
facilitating	organizing grand-children	organizing gardens	organizing golf	organizing travel	organizing home decor
initiating	initiating human potential	initiating family	initiating nature	initiating literacy	initiating beauty
creating, designing	creating, designing human potential	creating, designing family	creating, designing nature	creating, designing literacy	creating, designing beauty
inspiring	inspiring human potential	inspiring family	inspiring nature	inspiring literacy	inspiring beauty
mentoring	mentoring human potential	mentoring family	mentoring nature	mentoring literacy	mentoring beauty

I care about

Natural
roles I love

With the creating beauty idea in mind, for instance, I heard of a class called Art for the Non-Artist. That was right up my alley as I don't consider myself artistically inclined. I signed up and learned so many ways to create beauty in a non-threatening, empowering way. I now apply my new skills using water colours, inks, lettering, and design to create cards I give to the special people in my life. And to just play and be.

While contemplating creating/ designing human potential, I had the insight to create the Six Circles of Life model as a guide to life fulfilment.

With 25 ideas of your own, what intrigues you for future consideration? Rephrase it in a way that makes sense. Now you have a thought that can become a thing, a phrase Mike Dooley of www.tut.com uses. Dooley's exact quote is, *"Thoughts become things. Choose the good ones."*

....

....

....

Try different *roles I love/ what I care* about combinations until you discover something that you want to start exploring.

Live Your Legacy Now

What is a legacy?

Most people will agree that a legacy is a lasting gift, one that lives on beyond your life on earth. Often legacy is thought of as a gift of material treasures or money. When you think of tributes extolling the virtues of someone who passed away, you know that a legacy is much more than that. It is the contributions you made to family, friends, and society; the compassion, love, and kindness you showed others; the kind of person you were.

Considered in this context, what your life has meant to others is your legacy. Reb Zalman left such a legacy when he passed on in 2014. The profound new vision of growing older that he wrote and spoke about founded the growing Sage-ing International community www.sage-ing.org.

What about what your life means to *you now as you are living it?*

I propose that we don't wait to leave a legacy but to live it now. Why not live life today being our best selves with the highest purpose for the greatest good? Lofty sounding, I know. This does not need to be big. It can translate to living with joy and passion being who you are in your own space.

You are already living your legacy – just being who you are

In this context, a legacy is a lasting gift to the universe of your thoughts, words, and deeds – of your authentic self, expressed through living your passion and joy.

You are already living your legacy – just being who you are. Each of your thoughts, words or actions produces a reaction in someone else that can contribute to their well-being and self-esteem, or take it away.

Legacies are both inherited and created. The messages your parents and your culture instilled in you is one of their legacies to you.

"Where there's a will, there's a way" is a legacy passed on by my parents and likely their parents as well. If you really believe in something and want to make it happen, you will. Henry Ford famously said, *"If you believe you can or believe you can't, you're right."* What you believe becomes true, a self-fulfilling prophesy.

The idea that thoughts become things has been around for centuries. It gained new awareness in more recent years with Rhonda Byrne's *The Secret*, Wayne Dyer's *Change Your Thoughts, Change Your Life*, and through the works of many other thought leaders. Where attention goes, energy flows. That is how it all happens.

Where attention goes, energy flows.

Legacies are both inherited and created.

Knowingly, or unknowingly, you have already created a legacy with the deeds, messages and beliefs you passed on to your family, friends, and through your paid or community work. You are now poised to continue that legacy and seize the opportunity of long life, long health, and long usefulness to grow that legacy or create a new legacy and... to live that legacy now.

What do you want to live your life for? What difference do you want to make in your own small corner or a bigger one? How do you want to be true to who you are, use your talents, and make your own contribution to the greater good?

Here are some examples of how others are creating and living a legacy.

Making a difference

My sister Joanne has an Authentic Blue/Organized Gold temperament blend with a passion for anything medical and for people who have little family support nearby. She has created a role for herself as a friendly visitor, a driver, and an advocate for frail elderly people as they negotiate their way through the health care system. She does this as a volunteer on her own and through her church connections. At 75 and with compromised health herself, this is something she is physically and mentally able to do. She has found a meaningful way to live with purpose and make a difference to others in her circle.

Passionate about animals

Elaine, 72, Organized Gold, is a pet lover. She owns two dogs and a cat and fosters dogs referred to her by the animal shelter in her community on a temporary basis. Elaine is also the coordinator of volunteers in a therapeutic dog program, interacting with and scheduling volunteers and their dogs to organizations in the program. Her passion for animals has found a useful niche in the community where therapy dogs are making a significant difference to individuals, from students with exam anxiety to behaviourally challenged children to anyone who could use some unconditional love.

And so on

Peter, 64, Resourceful Orange, was a pilot who retired involuntarily according to company policy at 55. After living the initial years of retirement savouring his freedom while missing his job, he began to feel the urge to contribute to his community, but only on his own terms. After trying several options, he is now mediating neighbour disputes in a program that accommodates his need for making a casual, not regularly scheduled, contribution to his community.

Diana, 68, Inquiring Green/ Resourceful Orange, loves to design wearable art out of gemstones, fabric, or yarn. As a grandmother, she has found a home for her creations with an organization that raises funds to support grandmothers in Africa who are raising their orphaned grandchildren on their own. Her art has a lasting impact and is a legacy worn and enjoyed by many people.

Marilyn, 65, Authentic Blue, sold the corporation she owned and now works part time in a home-based business facilitating workshops for those preparing for retirement. She volunteers in her community as a drum circle facilitator leading healing energy sessions through the rhythm and vibrations of the drums.

When Richard, 75, Organized Gold, retired, he moved to a community in southern France where he converted and renovated a centuries-old farmhouse into a tourist accommodation. Richard combined this seasonal business with a volunteer consulting role for an international organization, lending his expertise to countries interested in protecting their natural areas.

Stuart, 67, Inquiring Green, a semi-retired IT specialist serves on the board of a community service agency he cares about, contributing his strategic long range vision talents to ensure the organization's survival and growth.

Bruce, 71, Inquiring Green, retired from an engineering career at 52 to buy an existing business he had frequented as a hobbyist, making many other hobbyists happy to see the business continue and expand.

Ted, 68, Inquiring Green/ Authentic Blue, is a medical professional who continues to work in his own practice doing what he loves. Each year he travels to another country to volunteer his medical skills to those-in-need.

Bill, 73, Resourceful Orange/ Authentic Blue, has been in the process of building his dream home in the wilderness for many years. First visualized in his youth, the building of it is the actualization that Bill is now living in the middle of a natural area he's passionate about. Bill has planted a personal tree for each of his grandchildren, the trees growing up along with the grandkids.

Before he retired at 65, Ray, 80, had created a seasonal farm for himself that involves the whole family, a legacy he has enjoyed living for more than 15 years and one he plans to leave for his children and grandchildren when he passes on.

Here are more examples to help get you thinking:

Dolores loves to line dance and belongs to a group that teaches and demonstrates line dancing to residents in retirement homes. No partner required. Al brings a sing-along gang to sing with residents in retirement communities. Elly and Roger teach English as a second language on contract overseas. Desiree sews and donates warm wraps to a seniors' shelter. Sheila is a contract health care professional helping emerging countries develop a public health system. Jeannette helps emerging cultures develop sustainable agriculture practices. Margaret works during national and provincial elections as a returning officer.

Kathryn loves to read and volunteers by recording articles for people with limited or no eyesight. Eileen volunteers her accounting skills on behalf of a political candidate she supports. Robert delivers campaign literature and makes calls to support his preferred candidate. Bill does audits for an international organization. Leo organizes fundraising events for a local charity. Audrey bought a virtual franchise that promotes and sells healthy living products. Els volunteers part time in a hospice as a companion/ caregiver. Fran sews a new pillowcase for each woman sheltered in a temporary home. Brenda teaches reading skills to low-literacy children in school. The contributions in these examples are priceless and not easily measured. Each makes a difference to someone – and leaves a legacy that contributes to the greater good of each individual that spreads out to society as a whole.

Do whatever you do with the bigger picture in mind – what is its purpose?

The story of two bricklayers – a popular legend

A traveller came upon two men smoothing concrete between the layers and sides and expertly fitting each brick into place.

He asked the men what they were doing.

"I'm laying bricks," answered the first man.

"I'm building a cathedral," answered the second.

Each was doing exactly the same job using the same skill set. Their perspective, however, was completely different. One was doing a task. His colleague saw how his work contributed to a much bigger picture. He was creating a cathedral!

Do whatever you do with the bigger picture in mind – what is its purpose? How is it contributing? Whatever you do will not seem meaningless when you understand how it's contributing to the greater good.

Whatever you do will not seem meaningless when you understand how it's contributing to the greater good.

BE the Change Spiral

The BE the Change Spiral is a tool to define your own contribution to society by satisfying one of your values and applying your skills and talents to a cause you believe in. Use the spiral to let your contribution ripple out into the world in the mysterious ways you won't even know about.

BE the Change Spiral

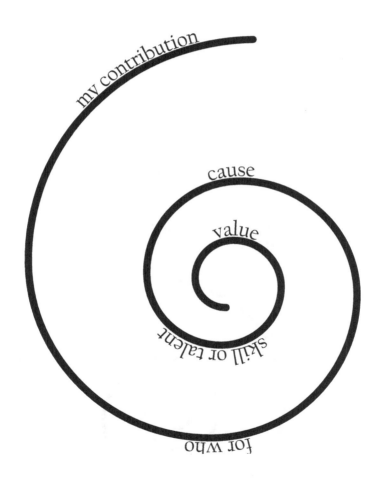

Making a difference in a new community

When they retired, Bill and Nancy moved from a city to a rural community with a rich cultural heritage. They embody the Be the Change Spiral, following their values, skills, and talents to contribute to a cause they believe in.

Values – concepts, ideas, challenge, innovation, and intellect

Skill or talent – researching, initiating, organizing, and mobilizing

Cause – enhance respect for and preserve the culture and history of my community

For who – everyone from locals to visitors and from children and youth to adults and seniors

Contribution – create an annual event that celebrates local music, food, culture, and language

The change – a greater recognition and appreciation by all for our community's rich cultural roots.

 Start in the centre of the spiral by identifying and writing one of your values – perhaps the one you most want or need to satisfy now. Refer to *Chapter 2: Be Who You Are* – Values Clarification Tool.

Moving out from the centre, add one of your natural skills or talents from *Chapter 6: Be a Contributor*, pages 110-111 – any of the data, people, things, and ideas – being as specific as you can.

Continuing outward, select a specific cause you care about and who (individual, group, age, demographic, setting) you want to focus on (from *Chapter 5: Be Compassionate*, p.82-84).

Then identify a more specific contribution you want to make.

A couple's contribution to community theatre

Gisela values creativity. Her skills and talents include acting, singing, leading, and directing. The cause she believes in is giving everyone an opportunity to be involved in and enjoy theatre locally including actors, stage managers, set, sound, lighting, costume, and prop design and maintenance, and the audience who's exposed to and enjoys quality productions. Gisela's contribution is directing a play each year, contributing to community spirit, connectedness, sense of well-being, and joy.

Joe values contributing. He is skilled at working with tools and equipment, wood and other materials. Joe volunteers at the amateur theatre community group creating props, scenery, and maintaining the theatre building throughout the year. He and his fellow volunteers enjoy meeting once a week for a cup of coffee while planning and implementing their projects. Joe is contributing in his own way to community spirit, connectedness, sense of well-being, and joy.

Here is how my own example evolved.

My top value is the need to be useful – to contribute to society in a meaningful way. The transferable skills I have and love are creating and facilitating. Catalyst roles come most naturally to me. I care most about human potential, specifically the potential of people who in later life are not sure what they can do with their lives. Contribution Statement – I want to inspire individuals to know their options for living fully being who they are, to use their talents and wisdom for the greater good, to be the change they wish to see in the world in whatever way that is meaningful to them personally.

In your Spiral, play with the words and the meanings. Mix and match different skills, causes and roles. Write simply in your own words. Put it aside overnight and look at it again the next day or next week until you feel you have it, until you feel this is one way you can be a contributor. I revised the wording of my own contribution statement many times and will doubtless do so again.

Reflections:

🌀 In your journal, write your thoughts and feelings about the Spiral exercise

🌀 Review your Spiral's components

🌀 Draft a contribution statement

🌀 Edit and revise as you wish

Your contribution statement

....

....

....

In *Appendix A* or your journal, write how you want to be a contributor
You likely don't know how to implement your ideas exactly. No worries. In the next chapters you will discover perspectives and tools to experiment and start making your ideas more real.

The BE the Change Spiral can be considered a tool to know a purpose for living, to create meaning, or to live *now* a legacy you want to create – in your own unique way. To know one or more reasons you are here and how, with the gift of longevity, you can contribute to a better world. There IS a reason that is yours to discover. It is well worth exploring no matter how long it takes. Life is a journey after all, not a destination. Make this quest your journey.

CHAPTER 7

BE CURIOUS

"The mind is like a parachute. It functions only when it's open."

Source unknown

Be Curious is about this open mind – to continuing to learn something. It's about the relationship of challenge and boredom and about how to use curiosity to discover the information you need to make your ideas a reality.

Mental decline is not inevitable!

The brain continues to amaze us with its neuroplasticity, a plasticity that has overturned the old doctrine of the unchanging brain. At the frontier of brain science, Norman Doidge, M.D., proves in his book *The Brain that Changes Itself* that:

- a damaged brain can often reorganize itself so that when one part fails, another can often substitute

- if brain cells die, they can at times be replaced

- many 'circuits' and even basic reflexes that we think are hardwired are not

- it is possible for 80-year-olds to sharpen their memories to function the way they did when they were 55

Jill Bolte Taylor's personal story of the neuroscientist's stroke that obliterated the left side of her brain and the ultimate restoration of her left brain functions is one example of this amazing neuroplasticity. Watch Taylor tell her inspiring story on www.TED.com, one of TED's most popular talks, or read her book, *My Stroke of Insight*. Check out TED's other informative 18-minute talks on every imaginable subject by the world's experts. Better than watching television, some say.

With new brain discoveries discussed by experts like Doidge and Taylor, we can look forward with the hope that what we think and do today can help keep our brains stimulated and functioning for a long time. Mental decline is not inevitable! Cognitive skills can actually increase with age. That is the hopeful message of this chapter with its ways to keep being stimulated.

The key is to be curious

The key is to be curious – inquisitive, interested, intrigued, questioning. It is the natural domain of the Inquiring Green personality temperament. Greens' favourite question is "why" – followed by "how" and "what"? We all have some green in us and this is the place to dust it off, polish it up, and let it shine.

Be curious to:

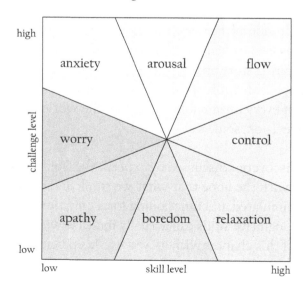 help keep brain neurons connected and to create new connections

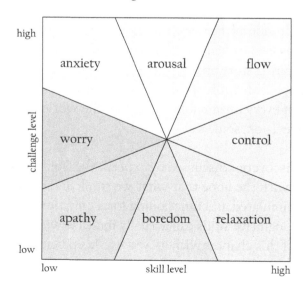 avoid boredom

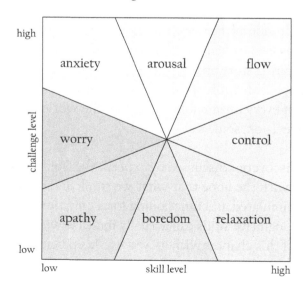 discover answers to your questions

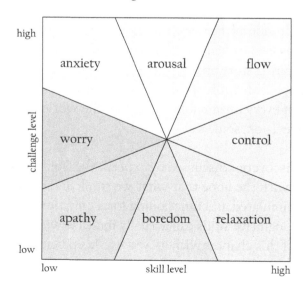 keep learning, exploring, and discovering

I became intrigued 15 or more years ago when a friend, Peter Heron, told me about the work of his former colleague at the University of Alberta, Mihyali Csikszentmihalyi (Peter called him Mike), who had drawn a connection between skills, challenge, boredom, and flow. He referred me to Mike's book, *Finding Flow, the Psychology of Engagement with Every Day Life* with the following chart, used here with permission.

Notice the left axis is CHALLENGE moving from LOW level in the bottom left corner to HIGH level in the upper left corner.

The row at the bottom axis is SKILLS, moving from LOW level in the bottom left corner to HIGH level in the bottom right corner.

When you no longer have challenge and use only your lowest level skills, apathy or boredom can be the result. When you have some challenge and use higher level skills, relaxation and control result. Too much challenge with few skills to meet them results in worry and anxiety. Just the right amount of challenge for you combined with the right amount of skills results in arousal or stimulation. At the highest level of challenge and skills, flow results.

I was particularly interested in where boredom is located on the chart: low on the challenge axis and in the middle on the skills axis.

This Finding Flow Chart explains so much. This could, for example, explain why some people say they're bored when they retire. They will rarely admit it to others, as they're supposed to be busy and enjoying retirement, but that's not the case for everyone. Financial advisors and my own experience confirms boredom is more common than we might have thought. Perhaps taking on more challenge or using higher skills is a solution to boredom?

Apathy: Low skills and low challenge – you're going through the motions of living.

Boredom: Middle skills and low challenge – while occasional boredom is normal, chronic boredom is an invitation for a new challenge.

Relaxed: High skills and low challenge – you may prefer living life here.

Control: High skills and medium challenge – you're coasting.

Worry and Anxiety: High challenge and low skills – stress.

Arousal: Middle skills and middle challenge – stimulation.

Flow: High challenge met by high skills – optimum experience.

How To Find Flow

We do not live in flow mode all of the time – it's found only on those occasions when we are stimulated to take on a challenge in which we discover our skills are up to the task. We're focused. When I'm creating something, for instance, I'm in a flow state. When I'm facilitating, I'm in a flow state. The rest of the time I can be in any of the other states, including relaxed, or in control, and sometimes even a little bored. I've experienced worry and anxiety, too, though I choose not to be there for long – the option is to either decrease the challenge or increase the skill level.

Runners, swimmers, and other athletes are in a flow state when they are 'in the zone'.

One way to know you're in flow is that time seems to stand still – you're not aware of it at all. I can forget to take breaks, forget to eat. Hours go by until I surface again and I'm surprised when I look at the clock and discover the hours that have passed. There are whole perspectives on space and time that you may find interesting to learn more about, such as how does time travelling work? You may discover some interesting ideas.

Have an open mind to exploring something you don't know just yet.

 Think of times when you experienced flow in the past and times when you experience flow now, when you're challenged and using your highest skills.

Write about these experiences in a notebook or journal. It's joyful to relive these experiences this way.

You can create more stimulating and flow experiences in the future! It's not too late. Don't allow yourself to linger in apathy and boredom for long. Have an open mind to exploring something you don't know just yet. Be curious.

Informal Learning

Creating a website

Victor, an old school and university chum, had been retired for a few years when we caught up with him again. He updated us about his life and his love for golf. I asked him if there was anything he felt was missing and he replied, "I could use more challenge." With a somewhat mischievous smile, I challenged him to do something more than send a Christmas card with only his signature on it as his annual communication with us. The following Christmas, to our amazement, Victor had created a personal website to share. In subsequent years, he scanned and added old photos, videos, and blogs. He found and enjoyed a new challenge and taught himself new skills in the process.

Victor's story shows that adding a new challenge and continuing to learn does not need to be formal. It can be informal, too.

Here are other ways to learn informally.

The travel challenge

Each time Tom and I travel someplace new, we are reminded of the amount of challenge and learning involved in researching and planning the trip – where to go, what to see and do, where to stay, how to get around. Going to the same location, booking an all-inclusive resort, or taking a cruise or tour makes all that a bit easier as much is done for you once you've researched the cruise or resort. If you want a relaxed vacation, choose this way to go. If you want more challenge, make all your own arrangements.

Those with an Organized Gold temperament may prefer the cruise or organized excursion way of travel. Or they may prefer to plan everything themselves to the last detail, including creating an Excel spreadsheet of their plans. At the very least, the bookends need to be in place (where to stay when you arrive and depart and how you'll get there) and some components to feel in control. Chantelle and Roger chose a different way. They sold their house and bought a mobile home to travel and see the world. This way of travel may appeal to those with a Resourceful Orange temperament. They may also like adventure travel such as non-guided biking or hiking vacations, scuba diving adventures, or caving.

Inquiring Greens often prefer an educational component to their travels – to learn the history, geography, flora, fauna, culture, or language of the area they are visiting. A bird watching trip or museum tours may also be up their alley. Many universities offer study/ travel programs that involve attending classes with fellow travellers who then all travel together to the chosen destination with the instructor as a guide. Also look into Road Scholar www.roadscholar.org and Routes to Learning www.routestolearning.ca that offer travel combined with seminars by local experts.

And Authentic Blues may want to meet local people and learn about a culture first hand. They may enjoy voluntourism – a combination of travel and charity work to immerse themselves in the culture and make a contribution at the same time. They can check out www.voluntourism.org, www.voluntourism.ca, and Google voluntourism to discover other organizations that combine travel and making a difference on every continent of the world meeting the needs of diverse populations.

Informal learning closer to home

- Be a tourist in your own community and visit the sites tourists come to see.

- Learn a new skill – a musical instrument, another language, a game, a sport, a craft.

- Start a new hobby or expand your skills in an existing one.

- Attend a meet-up in an area of interest, meet new people and learn about the group's activities.

- Attend fairs and exhibitions.

- Attend a public lecture at your library or anywhere.

- Buy a library membership and borrow books, music, and movies.

- Buy a mobile device to read ebooks and articles, and stay on top of the news.

- Watch documentaries and newscasts – try a channel new to you from anywhere in the world.

- Listen and watch TED Talks – learn about anything online or on TV from the best in the world.

- Switch household tasks with your partner – learn a new skill.

- Start or change an exercise program – engage a personal fitness trainer to get you started on the right track.

- Start a different way of eating and learn the ins and outs plus a bunch of new recipes.

- Join a choir or band and learn new musical scores.

- Join a line dancing group and learn the sequence of a new dance each week.

๏ Be creative, creativity stimulates the brain. Use any medium – art, music, drama, writing, crafts, design, dance.

๏ Start your own business from home.

๏ Be innovative – create a new invention, a different way of doing things.

๏ Do puzzles, play games.

๏ Use online brain tools to stimulate the brain to solve problems.

 Try this classic nine-dot puzzle that I've often used with groups to stimulate thinking before facilitating a brainstorming or visualization exercise.

Directions: Connect all nine dots with four straight lines, drawn without lifting pen from paper or retracing a line.

This is definitely not easy. Use creative, out of the box type thinking to help solve this puzzle.

The solution is in *Appendix F*. Don't peek until you've tried it for at least three minutes.

Many more and both easier and more difficult brain stimulation tools and games can be found online and on mobile apps. Try luminosity www.luminosity.com as one example that helps keep those neurons of yours connecting! Because online anything to excess can become obsessive or addictive, be cautious. Be sure to include activities in the other circles

– N.E.A.T. activities from *Chapter 4: Be Well* and strategies from *Chapter 5: Be Compassionate* to avoid isolating yourself from society.

Formal Learning

Formal learning involves registering in a credit or non-credit course or seminar offered through a community college, a university, a corporate, government or non-government training program, or a private educational entity, participating either in person or online.

New skills for bed and breakfast

Amy participated in a career planning workshop I was facilitating. She excitedly told me that when her husband retired in six months, they were moving to a Caribbean island where they were building a bed and breakfast inn. Having already left her paid position, she was in the workshop to figure out what she could do in the six-month interval. Through the career planning process, Amy came to realize she was missing an essential skill set to operate the new business: accounting skills. It suddenly became completely clear what she needed to do in the next six months. Amy enrolled in several accounting courses to prepare herself for her upcoming role.

No more required learning

Joe enrolled in a whole range of general interest classes at his nearby university when he retired. He revelled in the freedom of learning something that had nothing to do with his former work and everything to do with being enlightened in a subject of interest. This included learning the basics of the language of his future daughter-in-law to prepare himself for meeting her parents in their own language. Joe discovered the additional benefit of interacting with people of all ages in the classes he attended.

Besides taking a class in person from any post-secondary institution, you can take courses online right from home. Some of these are free. Coursera, www.coursera.org, for example, offers free courses in a whole range of subjects for credit or non-credit. Have a look and be surprised at what experts are offering free of charge.

Here are more ways to learn something new and stimulate the brain at the same time.

- Take individual lessons from a teacher in an interest area you want to learn – guitar, dance etc.

- Attend a continuing education class offered by secondary and post-secondary institutions. Check out their catalogues for a large array of classes in just about every possible subject you may be interested in.

- Attend a conference or seminar offered through an organization you belong to.

- Speak at such an event yourself.

- Join the lifelong learners association in your area. Attend a short course and perhaps teach a course yourself.

- Join an organization such as Toastmasters International to learn public speaking skills and lead meetings.

- Attend learning and development sessions offered through any group. In my city of Calgary, for instance, there is an organization for women to learn about issues specific to women's health and well-being.

- Finish that degree you've always wanted to have. Or enrol in a certificate or diploma program. Eighty-somethings are doing it, and so can you if that's what you would enjoy.

- Get certified in a skill that is useful in your work now or in the future. Add tools to your toolkit.

- Take a look at the University of the Third Age www.U3A.org.uk.

- Informal and formal learning challenges stimulate the brain.

What Are You Curious About?

Which of the ideas you've interested in do you want or need to know more about?

....

....

....

What information and resources do you want to consult?

Highlight items in the *References and Resources* section at the back of the book to begin your research.

Write other resources you know or learn about here:

....

....

....

This is the start. Be open to experiment and to keep adding new resources as one thing leads to another.

Talk to people. Ask everyone you know or meet if they know someone or a resource that could help you. Use the 5 W's and how: WHO, WHAT, WHEN, WHERE, WHY, and HOW. This is not prying if done sincerely and respectfully. Think of this as a research project to learn what you need in order to make an informed choice.

....

Learn what you need in order to make an informed choice.

Open-ended questions that cannot be answered by a simple yes or no will yield the most information. For example, you could ask someone already doing what you're considering any of the following questions in your research:

- ⊙ What drew you to choosing this option?

- ⊙ How did you get into this?

- ⊙ What did you need to do to get started?

- ⊙ Where can I find more information?

- ⊙ What is it you find rewarding about it?

- ⊙ What is something you don't enjoy about it?

- ⊙ Why should someone like me be interested in doing this?

- ⊙ What should I do first?

- ⊙ Who else do you suggest I talk to?

The information you gain is invaluable. Be sure to thank them for their time and willingness to share.

Being curious will ensure you won't be bored. You'll keep your brain stimulated with cognitive functions firing on all cylinders. You'll live with joy and flow.

Keep going and design a meaningful future the Planned Happenstance way (*Chapter 8: Define a Direction*).

PART II

DESIGN YOUR

MEANINGFUL FUTURE

CHAPTER 8

DEFINE A DIRECTION

"If you can imagine it, you can achieve it."

Walt Disney

Planned Happenstance

John Krumboz, a respected career development theorist, developed the Planned Happenstance theory that I subscribe to. This theory suggests that when you create a vision or a direction for your life, define a short term goal to make it real, and take the first step, you are *setting in motion* a series of circumstances, serendipity, coincidences, happenstance, or whatever you want to call it, that will reveal resources and opportunities, even though the details of exactly *how* this will all happen are not clear when you start.

That is how Planned Happenstance works. Look back on your own life and see if this has been as true for you as it has been for me. Did you plan everything that happened in your life? The groups that I've posed this question to invariably reply, "No".

Evolving opportunities

Since I was a teen, I have always wanted to be in some sort of a helping profession. At first I thought I would like to become a social worker but a timely conversation with a favourite teacher who had switched from a social work to a teaching career changed my mind. Then I thought I would like to become a teacher but I was too scared to speak in front of a group, especially with another teacher there to evaluate me. Undecided, I completed an arts degree relying on the modern languages and psychology subjects I enjoyed to lead me to something of interest. Parenthood intervened and I focused on being a full time mom and part-time volunteer in my community using helping and leadership skills.

The desire for a helping profession never left and became more defined when I knew I needed to gain the confidence to speak to groups, something I knew to be a woeful inadequacy. For mostly selfish reasons, this translated into setting the intention and seizing an opportunity to instruct a college diploma course in written communication skills. With a great deal of ignorance, I believed I knew enough of the content basics that I could learn the necessary speaking skills. I still feel sorry for those early students who tolerated my own learning curve in this department. After surviving the first course, followed by six years instructing two courses per term with growing skill and confidence, my mission was accomplished and I was ready for the next challenge.

Now it became clear that I wanted to make a difference in a more meaningful way, through personalized workshops of longer duration with smaller, more intimate groups. And with no marking involved! I noticed an ad for this type of workshop and registered as a participant. I asked how I could lead such a workshop myself and was referred to the appropriate contact. Slowly and gradually, I became a workshop facilitator for adults interested in exploring new careers and learning work search skills. I discovered that facilitating came quite naturally to me. After learning the basics, I became totally comfortable being me and speaking to groups with confidence and some say, wisdom. Career development became my passion! My intention from midlife on has been to inspire others to live a fulfilled second half of life, initially through creating the Retire to the Life You Design workshop, tools, models, and a workbook to support this and then through training other trainers who approached me to do this work.

My intention now is to share what I know and learned with you through these pages – still in the same direction but with a new short term goal and, yes, a new challenge and continued learning.

Did I know in advance I would be doing what I am today? Not really – all this evolved in surprising ways as I followed a direction, identified parameters, set the intention to make it a reality, asked questions, took an action, and seized an opportunity. New, unexpected opportunities followed.

John O'Donohue, a wise theologian, expressed this idea beautifully:

"I love to live like a river flows, carried by the surprise of its own unfolding."

The *surprise* of its own unfolding!

As a river journeys in a direction, sometimes around obstacles, through easy channels, over rapids, sometimes fast, sometimes slow, sometimes resting in pools or lakes for a while, it eventually carries on in the direction of its intended course. And so it is with us.

Identifying Your Direction

Perhaps your own life journey, like a river, suggests a general direction (a pattern or a theme) you have been moving in all along. Perhaps you have been temporarily sidetracked or lost sight of the pattern, but now you can see its direction again.

In addition to the BE the Change Spiral Tool in *Chapter 6: Be a Contributor*, two additional tools can help you identify the direction you want to move in.

1. The Life Review Tool invites you to look to your past to discern a direction you may wish to continue.

2. The Visualizing Your Future Tool invites you to explore what is possible in your future.

 Life Review Tool

If a theme or direction is not obvious to you, it's very helpful to do a life review using this chart. Think in terms of seven-year intervals or any intervals that make sense to you and your life experience. For me, the locations I lived in made the most sense to use. For you, it may be decade markers.

What were the significant experiences, achievements, and challenges in any of the areas of your life? Write these here or in your journal.

Self Home Family School Work Leisure Community	Age 0-7	8-14	15-21	22-28	29-35
36-42	43-49	50-56	57-63	64-70	71-77
78-84	85-91	92-98	99-		

Reflections

- ๏ Have some experiences repeated themselves, perhaps in different forms?

- ๏ Can you detect a pattern or theme?

- ๏ Can you see a general direction your life has moved in?

- ๏ Do you wish to continue in this direction?

- ๏ Is a new direction being revealed to you? Listen to your intuition – what is niggling at you? Don't ignore this!

If you wish, write your life story in narrative form. This is a very interesting and informative exercise. Give your story a title. See what I did with my story in the beginning pages of this book as one example – *Nell Ventures Into New Worlds*. Read autobiographies for other examples.

Visualizing Your Future Tool

Consider what is possible for your future. I have used this visualization exercise for years with thousands of people. Some find it easier to visualize than others. No matter, even a glimmer of an idea or a hint of something can provide the seed for ideas to sprout and bloom. Allow yourself to suspend judgment and let your thoughts go where they will.

Directions: In a quiet place where you can be uninterrupted for a while, sit comfortably in a chair, feet flat on the floor, and hands on your lap with nothing in them.

Take a deep breath in, following it through your nostrils right down to your belly, and back up and out again through the nostrils. Notice your belly naturally expanding and contracting as you breathe in and out. Repeat two more deep breaths, noticing its path in and out. You will want to lower your gaze or gently close your eyes to concentrate your awareness.

Now continue to breathe normally as you visualize a deep blue sky. Continue your normal breath.

Picture yourself getting on a magic carpet that takes you into the blue sky riding the currents like a bird, as far away or as close by as they take you. While on the magic carpet, know you have all the knowledge, wisdom, skills, and experience you need to be and do whatever you want. Nothing can stop you. No obstacles stand in your way. You have everything you need. You have permission and the freedom to be and do whatever you want. Continue to breathe to know and feel it inside you.

With that inner knowing, picture the magic carpet landing somewhere, close by or far away, a place where you can be truly yourself and do what you want. You get off the carpet and look around.

What do you see? Are you inside or outside? Pause to picture it.

What do you hear? Pause to hear it.

What do you smell? Pause to smell it.

What do you taste? Pause to taste it.

Are you alone or with someone? Pause. If with someone, is it one person, a group of people, or the public? Pause to be alone or with others.

What kind of clothes are you wearing to be who you are? Pause to be in those clothes.

What are you doing? Pause. What part of your body do you see yourself using? Is it your brain, your eyes, your ears, nose, voice, hands, legs, feet, your heart, your soul? Pause to do it.

How do you feel? Pause to feel it.

Now the magic carpet returns you to the present and the chair you're seated in. Gently open your eyes, move your toes and fingers, shake your hands and roll your feet, give your arms and legs a shake, gently move your head side to side.

While the picture is still fresh in your mind, draw a picture or write a paragraph describing it in as much detail as you can. Write in point form if you wish.

Beer on the beach

In his mind, John pictured himself on a beach operating a bar that served beer to thirsty sun worshipers. John loved beer himself, loved a warm climate, and loved being an entrepreneur operating his own business. These three ideas came together in this drawing with John serving happy customers, who were sitting on bar stools, with a big smile on his face, his feet planted in warm, soft sand while watching and hearing the incoming tide.

A healing retreat

Rhonda wrote this paragraph following the visualization exercise:

'I am in a log building with large windows looking out on a forest and lake. Inside is a group of people lying on yoga mats. I am wearing yoga clothes and am the yoga instructor who owns the retreat. I smell freshly squeezed orange juice. I hear mantras sung by Deva Premal and Miten. I feel relaxed and good about myself.'

A passion for cars

Mike jotted down these points after the exercise:

- *In my own garage*

- *Restoring a classic car*

- *Teaching a teenage boy*

- *Smelling wax, grease, and polish*

- *Listening to the Eagles*

- *I feel content and proud*

Reflections

- What does the future you visualized suggest to you?

- If you think it is impossible for you, don't push it away. Think of it as the seed of an idea to explore further. Discuss it with the important people in your life.

- Is there a piece of the idea that could be incorporated into your life? Perhaps not in the location you pictured but closer to home. One piece of it is better than no piece of it at all.

John thought attaining his beach-bar dream was likely not possible for him. Instead of discarding the idea outright, John could start by working for a time in a local microbrewery or a bar to test the experience and gain skills. He could plan a vacation to look into international living arrangements and business opportunities and see what evolved from that. He could have at least a piece of the dream right now. And who knows what could happen from there?

Define your direction.

After reflecting on the two tools, can you start to define a tentative direction? It can be in general terms or more specific. Below, or in your journal, write a draft direction sentence, draw a picture, or jot down a few points – try it here and now. Do not aim for perfection – whatever came into your mind is perfect. This is the point from which your river can start to flow in the natural direction it wants to, open to the surprise of its own unfolding.

Write a tentative direction here or in your journal:

CHAPTER 9

SET AN IMMEDIATE GOAL

AND TAKE AN ACTION

"Take a risk a day- one small or bold stroke that will make you feel great once you have done it."

Susan Jeffers

A goal has a name – it's more specific than your general direction.

When I moved back to Calgary after 32 years and entered the next phase of living fully, I put the word out to my professional network that I wanted to continue my passion for facilitating career planning and Retire to the Life You Design workshops – activities in the *Be Compassionate* and *Be a Contributor* circles.

In the *Be Well* and *Just Be* circles, I set out to find a community choir, join a book club, find a hiking group, learn Tai Chi and line dancing. By putting a name to these activities and communicating my intention to others, in very short order someone gave me the name of a Calgary contact that led to being able to continue the part-time contract work I loved. Finding a choir turned out to take numerous contacts and enquiries (this was in the days before online search engines) until a fit was found for both my husband and I. I met someone who invited me to join a hiking group though I hadn't breathed a word about that intention. I did mention I was looking for a book club and a new colleague invited me to a meeting of her book club. Next, I noticed an ad in my community newspaper for an introductory Tai Chi class in our neighborhood, as well as a beginners' line dancing class. Amazing! I have continued involvements with some of these, let go of others, and started other intriguing ones.

These activities all have a specific name – they are not abstract or nebulous. By naming them and taking action to explore and find them, the opportunities appeared.

Your Goals and the Life Balance Grid

Review the Six Circles of Life in *Appendix A* and the ideas you wrote in each circle.

Review the ideas you highlighted in the Interests, Skills, and Activities Sampler *(Appendix C)*. Review the Retirement Dimensions Sample Activities you highlighted *(Appendix D)*.

From these and any other ideas that have come to you, write a list naming everything you are interested in continuing, learning, trying, doing now or in the future. There are no limits – write 10, 20, 30 or 100 ideas.

Leave off the list activities that no longer suit your direction or purpose or are no longer of interest.

....

....

....

....

....

....

....

....

....

....

....

....

....

....

*Star the activities that most interest you to continue, do more of, or to start now or in the future. You will slot some of these into the Life Balance Grid.

The Life Balance Grid

The Life Balance Grid is a great planning tool to ensure you cover each of the Six Circles with at least one activity per week for mental, physical, and emotional well-being and for social connectedness.

 In the square that fits best write one of the activities you identified to continue doing, do more of, or start doing now or in the future.

Questions and Answers

- Do you want to do more than one activity per square? No worries, add them in.

- Did you find that some activities overlap? For sure – that is not at all uncommon. Try fitting in a different activity for each square, though, to enhance fulfilment and increase balance.

- Do you have any squares left blank? If so, that is an area to pay more attention to.

  Workshop participants most often find the bottom right square to be the most challenging – emotional and spiritual well-being. Think here of an activity that restores your energy, that you do to feel good and allows you to zone out for a while. Review the suggestions in the *Chapter 3: Just Be* and the ideas you wrote in that circle. Roger figured out that fishing, for him, fit this category, while for Linda it is gardening, and for Ted, hiking.

For the relationship with your partner or best friend square, Kathryn and her good friend Loreen joined a badminton club. They enjoy the weekly activity and a coffee visit with each other afterwards.

The Life Balance Grid

Activities to do:

Leisure	for fun or leisure	for work (paid or volunteer)	for learning or development
Work Learning			
Relationships	with my partner/ best friend	by myself	with family, friends, or others
& Social Connections			
Body	to keep fit	to stimulate my brain	for emotional and spiritual wellbeing
Mind Spirit			

Take An Action

Consider one thing you can do to start exploring your ideas a little further. There are really only four ways to explore something:

1. Reading about it – online, print or e-resources

2. Listening to a podcast, webinar, or watching a video.

3. Questioning others and learning from them. These can be people you know or people or resources others suggest that could inform you. Or they could be subject matter experts you find online or from whom you can take a tutorial, workshop, training seminar, or course, even free ones such as www.coursera.org.

4. Trying it – experiencing it for yourself.

I recommend starting with #1 and moving through #2, #3, and #4. Taking these easy actions will set in motion opportunities that become apparent seemingly through coincidences. The muddied waters become clearer. You come to realize you are being carried by the surprise of your own unfolding. Seize opportunities that feel right in your gut and move you in the direction you want to go towards. Planned happenstance is at work!

Recognize an opportunity when it presents itself AND take an action.

The trick is to recognize an opportunity when it presents itself AND take an action, as illustrated by the example in this old story.

He takes care of us

You may be familiar with the story, repeated here as I remember it, of the man who believed that God would take care of him at all times. When a massive flood was imminent and threatening homes, residents were urged to evacuate. The man refused, trusting that God would take care of him. As the waters began to rise, rescuers drove to his door to take him to higher ground. Again, he said no, God would take care of him. With the waters rising to the ground level of his home, the man watched from the second story as rescuers arrived in a boat to save him. Again the man declined – God would take care of him. Now on his rooftop, a helicopter was dispatched to take the man to safety, but he refused once again. Finally the man reached the pearly gates of heaven where he was met by God. The man was angry.

"I believed and trusted in you and you didn't take care of me at all!" he cried.

"Ah," said God, "I sent you a car, and a boat and a helicopter. Why did you refuse my help?"

Look for and notice patterns of opportunities that may appear as coincidences. One may be the opportunity you are hoping for. Commit to one action now to start exploring one of the new ideas in the Life Balance Grid to keep the momentum going.

Action	A Resource	Date to Start/Finish

The Bottom Line

- ◉ Define a general direction for your life.

- ◉ Take one action to explore that direction further. Write it in your organizer to do on a specific date.

- ◉ Don't stop after one action – keep going to the next one.

- ◉ Look for and *notice* opportunities.

- ◉ When an intriguing opportunity that fits your direction becomes apparent, grab it, even if it's short-term or temporary.

- ◉ Try it. You never know – this could be part of something that could lead to a more enduring involvement – or not.

- ◉ Repeat. Stay curious.

- ◉ Take action.

PART III

WHAT'S NEXT?

CHAPTER 10

UNDERSTAND THE

TRANSITION TO

RETIREMENT

"It's not so much that we're afraid of change or so in love with the old ways, but it's that place in between that we fear - it's like being between trapezes. It's Linus when his blanket is in the dryer."

Marilyn Ferguson

Change is an external event.

Transition is your emotional response to the external event.

Retiring from a job is change. Your emotional response is the transition. One does not happen without the other.

Change and transition are a normal part of living. You already have much experience – a job change, marital and family change, health change, housing change, location change. Through change, we grow and develop as human beings. If change had not happened, you would not be the person you are today.

Ask yourself what you learned from each change and what opportunities emerged that would not have been possible without the change.

I would not have met my husband if our family had not immigrated. I would not have had the incremental confidence-building experiences if we had not moved across the country ten times and I tried different leisure, learning, volunteer and paid work options. I would not have come to love others for who they are if we had not had two daughters and an adopted son, their partners, and our seven grandchildren, each with their own personalities, challenges, and special gifts. I would not have appreciated and respected each human being for their unique talents if I had not facilitated career/ life planning workshops. Though not all of these experiences were initially easy, each of the changes has helped me to be the person I am today and I am truly grateful for that.

You, too, have proven already that you are up to managing change and you can manage the one facing you now. The tools and resources on the following pages can help you prepare for this external event and your personal psychological response.

Voluntary and involuntary retirement

My husband, Tom, voluntarily chose to move on from his career at 55 when he took advantage of an offered exit package. Before he accepted, he prepared by attending the first Retire to the Life You Design workshop that I created for him and others like him – plus the thousands that followed. Freddi, 62, also retired voluntarily to new ventures she was fully prepared for. Even so, both Tom and Freddi, now working from home, had to adjust to the loss of routine, social connections, and the lack of separation between work and home. Being prepared, knowing compelling new options, and understanding the psychological transition to retirement, helped each of them through the process.

Nancy at 64 was shocked and angry when she was suddenly let go from a career she loved and valued. The blue chip company she worked for had decided to cut costs by letting its older and more highly paid workers go. Ed, at 54 was equally shocked when his company merged with another and his position became redundant. Highly specialized, Ed was not able to find new work in his field and felt he was involuntarily retired by the company.

Involuntary retirement is a psychologically more difficult transition than voluntary retirement.

In the four examples, the common element was the cessation of work as individuals knew it. The transition was each individual's personal, emotional response.

If a change is voluntary, like Tom and Freddi, you may feel excited by the new opportunities the change represents, even though there may be feelings of loss, fear, and anxiety accompanying it. If change is *involuntary*, like Nancy and Ed, you may initially feel anger, resentment, betrayal, and a profound sense of loss, often accompanied by a gripping fear. How will you cope? What will you do? What will others think?

Some participants in my workshops tell me they feel relieved. They may have been quite ready to move on but had not felt the energy to initiate the change themselves. Even though it was involuntary, relief was their dominant emotion now that it was a reality.

Understanding the Transition Process

William Bridges, in *Managing Transitions*, suggests there are three stages of transition that normalize the transition process. And it is a process – a process that can take anywhere from days, to weeks, to months, to even years, depending on your:

1. circumstances

2. resilience to change

3. preparedness

4. motivation to act

Understanding the three stages has helped thousands of workshop participants start to move from ending, to neutral, to new beginning stages of transition, from fear and confusion to hope, energy, and action. These were regular outcomes of the practical guidance facilitated through the workshop, available to you in the pages of this book.

The Transition Chart – 3 Stages of Transition

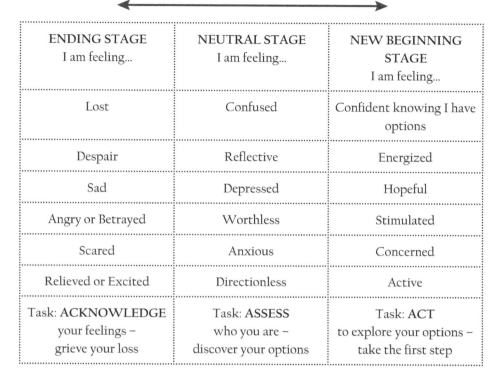

ENDING STAGE I am feeling...	NEUTRAL STAGE I am feeling...	NEW BEGINNING STAGE I am feeling...
Lost	Confused	Confident knowing I have options
Despair	Reflective	Energized
Sad	Depressed	Hopeful
Angry or Betrayed	Worthless	Stimulated
Scared	Anxious	Concerned
Relieved or Excited	Directionless	Active
Task: **ACKNOWLEDGE** your feelings – grieve your loss	Task: **ASSESS** who you are – discover your options	Task: **ACT** to explore your options – take the first step

Adapted from William Bridges, *Managing Transitions*

The Ending Stage

Here's what to expect when you cease working. In the first days, weeks, or even months of no work you may feel like you're on vacation – relieved at no more alarm clock, no more commute, no more stress. You are free at last from the external demands of work. Or, you may initially experience a sense of loss – of identity, purpose, routine, and social connectedness – a bit like a little lifeboat bobbing alone on the ocean with no shore in sight. You may also feel the loss of income and the safety and security work provided.

The first task is to acknowledge your feelings. They're common and normal – feelings shared by others just like you. Allow yourself to feel and grieve the loss of what was.

 In the Transition Chart, circle any or all the feelings in the ending stage that describe you.

Add any other feelings not on the chart. Write about these feelings in a journal. Be honest. This is just for you, not for others to read. Share only if you're comfortable with a trusted person. Know that it's okay to feel the way you do. In fact, it's entirely normal and expected. Go ahead and acknowledge your feelings.

How to Move from the Ending to the Neutral Stage

While acknowledging your feelings, you may come to realize that your former life is indeed over. What happened in the past is no longer in your control. There's nothing you can do to change it. You may still feel betrayed and angry, you may feel the loss of relationships and purpose, but it gets you absolutely nowhere to stay angry and lost. There's no point.

The key to moving to the Neutral stage is to ACCEPT that you cannot control or change what happened in the past. You cannot go back.

The only thing you can control is your RESPONSE to the change. You can choose to move forward and you can choose your attitude to the change. That is entirely in your power. No one can take that away from you. It is yours to decide.

When you come to realize that it's preferable to be better than bitter, you've moved to the Neutral Stage. You may still have days when you shift back to ending, and that's

The only thing you can control is your RESPONSE to the change.

normal, too. In time, you'll feel more and more ready to move forward with your life to the neutral and new beginning stages.

Do not skip the Neutral Stage!

The Neutral Stage

"When one door closes, another door opens." In the Neutral Stage, you are temporarily in the hallway with one door closed behind you, not knowing yet which new door will open.

Life in the hallway can actually become more confusing for a time. There are so many options! Should you follow what others in your circle are doing? Would you be happy there? Or are there options that are better suited to who you are, what you believe, and want you want for your own life?

 To begin, circle any or all the feelings in the Neutral Stage that describe you.

Add any other feelings not in the chart. Write about these feelings in a journal. Be honest. This is just for you, not for others to read. Share only if you're comfortable with a trusted person.

Nancy, who had been let go as a mature worker, sewed up a storm for a full week. She took all her anger and resentment out on her sewing machine and fabric creations. During the process, she was able to reflect on what had happened and gradually decided to close the door to the past and adopt a positive attitude. She realized there were actually new opportunities in her situation – many other doors to open. It wasn't all bad. She could choose now to indulge in her creative passions more fully, not knowing yet what specifically they would be and what they would lead to.

Ed, who had also found himself prematurely jobless, found solace learning all 108 moves of Tai Chi and through this meditative practice, worked through his emotions to neutral where he assessed what could be next for him.

Others may embark on a thorough house cleaning and de-cluttering, tackle that long awaited renovations project, or go on their dream trip. There's something about plunging into physical, meditative, or creative activities, or removing yourself from your home routine for a while that provides the conditions for the reflection and assessment necessary in the Neutral Stage.

Do not skip the Neutral Stage! It's a stage for affirming who you are not identified by your work – for identifying your values, interests, and skills, for exploring and experimenting with what can give your life renewed meaning, purpose, and direction. It is the space between identities.

Doing the Six Circles of Life exercises in this book are the perfect way to work through the Neutral Stage of Transition. You may be surprised at what's possible. And don't limit yourself to what you know now. Discover new options that may fulfill you in ways you could not have imagined!

How to Move from the Neutral to the New Beginning Stage

Confirming a tentative choice

Andy, 64, wanted to keep working at something when he qualified for his pension in one year. Because none of his co-workers felt the same way, Andy thought working was perhaps not an acceptable retirement choice. He became unsure about his options. When he attended our retirement preparation workshop, Andy told us that doing the Six Circles of Life, "Set me free!" For the first time, he was not confused but confident about his choices and ready to take action. What a relief that was for him and how stimulated, energized, and hopeful he became!

Setting a short-term goal

Ed decided to climb Mount Kilimajaro. This involved months of training during which he became more fit and healthier than he had been in a long time. The experience gave him energy and confidence to move on to further new experiences.

The New Beginning Stage.

To begin, circle any or all the feelings in the New Beginning Stage that describe you. Add any feelings not on the chart. Write about these feelings in a journal. Be honest. This is just for you, not for others to read. Share only if you're comfortable with a trusted person.

If, in doing this exercise, you find yourself circling back to some of the emotions in the ending or neutral stages, that's perfectly normal. You will have days when you're more confident and days when you're unsure, and days when you feel that loss still. That's why above the Transition Chart an arrow points left and right. It's also why the lines between stages have open spaces. It is part of the process to feel shifting emotions among the three stages. External events in non-work related parts of life also impact these emotions.

Increasingly, though, you will find yourself more in one stage than another. You're beginning to feel more confident, hopeful, and energized. Like Andy, you're ready to take action!

Taking the first steps to following your direction

By participating in our first workshop, Tom decided he would love to use more of his mediation skills. He was not yet sure how he was going to make this work, but now knew the direction he wanted to go. He would start by taking the courses necessary to obtain a certificate in mediation and join a professional association. To get experience mediating, he would volunteer for a community mediation program. All he had to do was to take the first step in the direction of this choice and be open to the opportunities that would inevitably emerge. Post training and diverse experiences, what emerged was Tom's election as president of the community program, president of the regional professional association, plus being a coach for mediation training programs. He has received a national award recognizing his contributions. You just never know what can happen post pension and the new ways you can contribute and be the change you wish to see in the world.

The task in the New Beginning Stage is to explore resources and take that crucial first step. To just do it! The second step will become evident with the information you glean and the people you meet by taking the first step. You may already know two or three steps. Be curious and open to possibilities and the rest will follow.

Here's what Nancy says about her new beginning, "My passion is quilting and I am proud of what I have accomplished post-employment in a corporate setting. The kudos I get for my quilts both traditional and art create warmth in my soul. My own satisfaction in constantly learning and growing is a blessing."

Tools for Your Transition

"The power of the mind and the spiritual forces surrounding us are always there for us to use, day to day, moment by moment, in every situation. If we find ourselves full of self-doubt, or if we want to accomplish something new that frightens us, we can access these powers."

Silken Laumann, Olympic medal holder, in her book *Unsinkable*

Eight Fear Busting Strategies

Fear, and its cousin anxiety, is one of the major obstacles to embracing change. It is a bigger obstacle than time, money, health, other people, and obligations. Even with all the time in the world and a secure source of income, fear can cripple a person from life fulfilment, from casting off from the safety of shore into uncharted waters. Doing nothing feels so much safer. The risk in doing nothing is to start on the slippery slope of shrinking your world to the four walls surrounding you. It could lead to boredom and loneliness, to having the TV and computer as your primary companions, to feelings of uselessness.

Time and again I have seen people pick themselves up and break free from the black hole of fear. If others can do it, so can you. If fear is what's stopping you, bust free with these strategies.

1. **Name that fear.** Much fear comes from a nameless resident that's made itself at home somewhere in your mind and body. You don't really know what it is you're afraid of and so it remains anonymous and debilitating.

    Some of the most common fears are fear of the unknown, fear of failure, fear of rejection, fear of not being good enough, fear of uncertainty, fear of ridicule, fear of loss, fear of not having enough money, fear of aging prematurely, fear of illness, fear of ending a relationship, fear of making the wrong decision, fear of uselessness, fear of dying, fear of loneliness, fear of boredom.

    What are you afraid of? Name your fear and stare it in the face. Make it reveal itself. Naming your fear is in itself a freeing experience.

    ....

2. **Ask yourself what if?** "What if my fear becomes reality? What is the worst that can happen?" Think this through. Picture it. Write it down.

    ....

    ....

    Now ask, "If it should happen, *how* would I handle it?" Rather than being afraid and hoping it won't happen, *create* a plan for the potentiality.

    ....

    ....

    The fear is really that we believe we can't handle what might happen. Naming it, preparing for it, and making a plan to handle it, reduces much of the fear.

Try this with something not earth shattering but concerning to you.

See how it works.

The wedding planner

I tried this strategy first in helping my elder daughter and son-in-law plan their wedding (yes, I could have been the stereotype of the future son-in-law's dreaded mother-in-law). I knew there were likely to be unknown gremlins waiting to thwart our best-laid plans – gremlins not in our control. I made a decision that I would not let these unexpected situations affect our enjoyment of the day. That was something I could control. So when two things did not go according to the perfect plan, I was ready. I did not allow them to upset me (as they may have if I had not already planned my response), calmly dealt with the situation, and the day turned out to be fun and stress-free for me and everyone else. Preparing to handle the unknown potential scenarios really worked!

---

3. **What if it doesn't happen?** Ask yourself "What if my fear does NOT become reality? What or how would I feel?"

    ....

    How would I act if it didn't become true at all? What would I do?

    ....

90% of what we worry about actually never happens. F.E.A.R. is an acronym for False Expectations Appearing Real.

Why worry needlessly? With strategy #2, you are ready with a plan for a 10% possibility.

Allow yourself to feel and act as if what you fear is NOT real, at 90% a much more likely possibility. Bulge those four walls just a little and take a small risk to begin. You have nothing to lose and everything to gain.

4. **Test your beliefs.** Byron Katie, in her book *Loving What Is: Four Questions That Can Change Your Life* suggests asking yourself these four questions to deeply and honestly consider the beliefs and thoughts that stop you from moving forward:

- Is it true?

- Can you absolutely know that it's true?

- How do you react, what happens, when you believe that thought?

- Who would you be without the thought?

Then turn the thought around. Find at least three specific, genuine examples of how each turnaround is true in this situation.

You can apply the four questions and the turn around to anything stopping you, including fear, relationships, work, goals, doubts, and self-limiting beliefs.

What if you were looking for work?

Let's try it with a thought common to many people. The 'I' in this example can be you or anyone.

Employers won't hire older workers like me.

- Is it true? *I've sent out 50 resumes responding to ads and have had no interviews. So it's true.*

- Can I absolutely know that it's true? *I've heard about something called the hidden job market but I don't know anything about it. So maybe I'm not quite 100% sure.*

- How do I react when I think that thought? *I give up trying to look for work and feel hopeless.*

- Who would I be without that thought? *I am confident knowing I have the transferable skills an employerneeds. I present myself online and in person with passion and confidence, straight posture, an up-do-date groomed look, a ready smile, and a firm handshake.*

The turn around

I know a few former colleagues, friends, and family members who are doing part-time, casual, contract, temporary or project work. They're flexible to try different work options. I can talk with them about their work and how they got into it. I can learn about the hidden job market and how to access it. I can learn about and create an online professional presence and a winning resume. I know resources to help me. I know there is something out there for me and I'll do whatever it takes, even if it takes more than a couple of months.

See *References and Resouces – Chapter 6: Be a Contributor* for resources.

Apply Byron Katie's four questions and the turn around to any one of your doubts or self-limiting beliefs.

5. **Ask yourself "what if I do nothing?"** That may be an appropriate option to buy yourself some time. Perhaps you don't have to do anything for now – though not for too long.

    How would I feel if I do nothing for now?

    ....

    What could happen?

    ....

    If you like your answer, do nothing for now. Maybe you just need a time out. Not making a decision IS a decision.

    If you do not like your answer try one or more of the other strategies.

6. **Get answers to your questions.** The source of much fear is the unknown. The solution is to access sources of information and turn your unknowns into knowns – to make an informed choice.

Turn your unknowns into knowns.

My questions...

Sources of information...

Start by checking out resources throughout this book and in the appendix. Ask questions of people you know and meet. Be curious. Include people who are doing what you would enjoy.

When to retire

Sharon believed all the articles and ads about the increasing number of people who have not saved enough money for retirement. She believed she may never be able to stop working. Being single, she was truly afraid of a future living on the street as a bag lady.

Sharon was advised to consult with the pension personnel at work to calculate what her actual retirement pension would be at 60 and every year until 70.... She also was advised to check government pension plan payments such as the Canada Pension Plan and Old Age Security that she would be eligible for. And to consult with a financial advisor on the best use of the savings she had accumulated. After taking all these steps, Sharon discovered she could adequately cover her expenses if she retired at 67, as long as she remained frugal with her financial resources.

Equipped with this information, the fear was gone and Sharon could plan for her future with new optimism and a clear picture of her retirement income.

Don't muddle along in a sea of fear. Don't make assumptions and decisions in a vacuum. Get the information you need to make an informed choice. Resources are available to help you.

7. Feel the fear and do it anyway. So says Susan Jeffers in her highly readable and helpful book, *Feel the Fear and Do It Anyway*. Nudge your comfort zone a little. What is one small risk you can take to face your fear? Refer to any of the strategies in this section, largely informed by Jeffer's work, and other suggestions throughout the pages of this book.

    Get the information you need to make an informed choice.

    What is one small risk you could take?...

    The payoff is gaining confidence in your ability to handle change and transition.

    Sitting at home doing nothing for any extended period is a recipe for stagnation and an unfulfilled future.

8. Practise Retirement. You don't have to feel obligated to make a long term decision right now. Try anything short term. Read on for more specific ideas about practising retirement.

    Feel the Fear and Do It Anyway.

Two Ways to Practise Retirement

1. Short term

If you're considering moving to a different home or a new location, try renting at the new location first. Try it in different seasons, too, to see if you would be happy there longer term. Find out how easy it is to join groups and make friends. Some companies have arrangements for employees to take a sabbatical or to bank vacation time to take months-long breaks

from work. Take advantage of this opportunity to rent a place in the location you're considering. Some of you may be able to work remotely from anywhere in the world and practise the new location that way.
In the same way, you can practise any of your options by trying them short term.

Organized Gold personality temperaments, whose core needs are duty, responsibility, and belonging, may have the most difficulty with the concept of practising retirement – Resourceful Orange personalities, with freedom as a core need, the least. Consider any one of your retirement options a pilot or research project knowing there is no obligation to continue long term if you determine it's not right for you.

If you like it and enjoy it, do more of it. If you don't like it and don't enjoy it, abandon the project and move on to other interests. This is not failure; it is your freedom to choose.

The operative phrase in practising retirement is to TRY IT.

2. **Phase your retirement.**

Instead of ceasing work abruptly, gradually reduce your work days from 5 to 4 to 3, if possible. This is a win-win for both employers and employees. You keep contributing your knowledge, skills, and wisdom to the organization while, by being flexible, the employer can keep benefitting from your contributions much longer. You can mentor the new recruits coming on board, focus on a special project that needs attention, or contribute a specialized skill or knowledge that would be missing if you had left the organization.

The operative phrase in practising retirement is to TRY IT.

Phasing retirement may look like this:

part–time paid work,

part–time volunteer work, learn and play

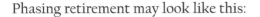

part–time volunteer work,

learn and play

To work part time, you can also consult, job share, do contract work, work from home, operate your own business, do casual, seasonal, or temporary work, or do unpaid volunteer work.

Phasing into retirement allows you meet your core needs and values while at the same time freeing you to explore the other options you would like to include in your life. Eventually you might stop paid work while other activities take centre stage.

The Retirement Continuum

Aging and retirement is a process we experience more than once – perhaps even three or four times.

In the first retirement, you are likely healthy, full of energy, and actively engaged pursuing your interests and passions. After a vacation break, you can't wait to get going again.

No-go is not retirement.

This stage could be what I earlier called the go-go pace that is most natural for your energy level.

After ten years or more, perhaps in your 70s or early 80s, you start to feel a reduction in normal energy levels. Mid-day naps may become appealing or necessary. Your body is showing its age with stiff and creaky joints, especially after sitting for a while. You function best at a more relaxed pace. You may decide to stop working now if you haven't done so already. This could be called the slow-go, relaxed stage, referred earlier to reduced energy levels.

In the slow-go stage, you experience another transition. It's time to let go of some activities and to review your earlier choices in the Six Circles of Life. It's time to plan what's next. You acknowledge your feelings, re-assess yourself, discover options, and act on the next step.

In the third stage of the continuum, health may be the biggest factor governing your choices. Perhaps you have experienced a major health event, you take longer to heal and recover, or you may no longer be as independent and self-sufficient as you once were. This is usually what scares people about aging and retirement. These factors are most common in the third stage, what could be considered the no-go stage when you no longer have the energy or health to be as active as you once were. Most people in this stage continue to live in their own homes, or a smaller version of it, perhaps with home maintenance or caregiving help from family, friends, or professionals. Fewer go to a care facility. Your days may consist of going to appointments with health care professionals. At this stage, an advocate may be necessary to help you navigate health systems, to speak and perhaps act on your behalf.

You may never experience the no-go stage, at least not until much later. No-go is not retirement. It is natural aging and a reality for all of us at some point.

There are of course outliers in these stages. While reading this you likely thought – this isn't true for my friend, my aunt, or myself. Individual situations, health, and energy levels vary. Depending on your situation, some of you may slow the pace much sooner or stay active much longer. Some of you have functioned on relatively low energy levels all your life and that won't change now. Others may need relief from the gruelling pace you've been on pre-retirement. The main point is that in general, most of us are not in no-go when we first retire – many are in go-go and some perhaps starting a move towards slow-go. So much is possible still to live the life you love with passion and purpose for the next 10, 20, or even 30 years, as long as you may have been in the workforce already!

Remember too that as we age, creativity, cognitive skills, spirituality, and wisdom increase. We don't just get older, we get smarter and wiser!

The transition to retirement is your opportunity to acknowledge your emotions, assess who you are, and act in a direction you want to move towards.

....

We don't just get older, we get smarter and wiser!

CHAPTER 11

FINAL THOUGHTS

"Never believe that a few caring people can't change the world. For indeed, that's all who ever have."

Margaret Mead

The next chapter of your life with its blank pages is ripe with potential for intentionally living the life you desire.

Use the Six Circles of Life framework as a guide, a roadmap to know the many options available to you. Use any of the tools, exercises, examples, and stories that are helpful to you in designing your own meaningful future.

Sharing these creations is my gift to you. I hope you will be inspired to nurture your personal well-being – physical, mental, emotional, social, and spiritual. Then, to use your unique talents and the gifts of long life and long health to better the world, one thought, one word, and one deed at a time – right where you are or choose to be, in your own authentic way.

Each thought, word and deed has its own energy, a force that ripples out to affect those near and far. We are all interconnected. Choose the good thoughts, the good words, and the good deeds and watch what happens. Be compassionate with yourself and others. Be a contributor. BE the change you wish to see in the world. That is the opportunity we have to make an individual and collective difference to society! That is how our lives have meaning and purpose.

A hymn from my childhood reminds me to:

"...be a little candle burning in the night. In this world of darkness, so let us shine, you in your small corner and I in mine."

This is the hope and the potential of a generation. How we already ARE part of the change that is starting to make the world a better place, one person at a time.

Contract with Self – write here what you want to commit to being or doing to live the life you love.

Post this contract on your mirror, fridge, or closet door. Write it in your daily calendar or as a smart phone note. Read it daily as a constant reminder.

....

....

....

....

....

....

My most positive thoughts and energy are with you as you live your next chapter with the meaningful future you have just set into motion!

APPENDICES

Appendix A: The Six Circles of Life

Record your personal findings here following the exercises in each chapter. If you need more space, use your notebook or journal.

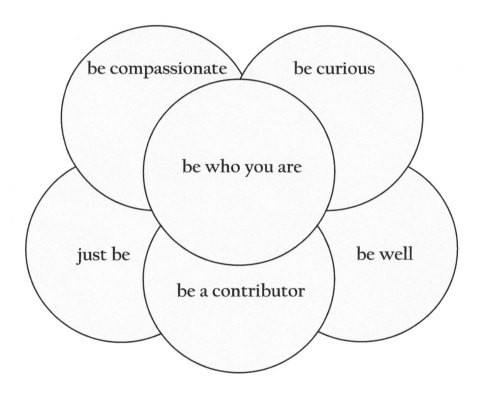

Appendix B: Your Circle of Self

Use highlighters or colouring pencils to illustrate the blend of colours most like you, a lot like you, somewhat like you and least like you from *Chapter 2: Be Who you Are.*

Appendix C: The Interests, Skills, and Activities Sampler

The sampler describes 10 interest and transferable skill categories with sample activities for each.

1. Highlight the categories in which you have some competency and/ or interest. If you have little competency now, no matter – you can learn whatever you're interested in!

2. Look at the second column for sample activities in each skill and interest category. Highlight all those that pique your interest.

3. Many of the activities can be done as paid Work, Volunteer work, or as Leisure activities. Place a W, V, or L beside the activity to keep track of your interest.

4. Write C for curious about to remind yourself to look into this further or to learn the skill.

Interests/Skills Categories	Sample Activities for Work, Volunteer, or Leisure
Helping People	• Taking care of children or youth. • Taking care of people who are frail, ill, or have a disability. • Helping people with their daily living needs such as shopping, cooking, banking, grooming, cleaning, or home maintenance. • Driving people to medical appointments (e.g., cancer patients needing treatments). • Teaching your skills or knowledge to others. • Tutoring students one-on-one. • Counseling others to help them solve their problems. • Advising or coaching others. • Mediating conflicts. • Mentoring others. • Being a spokesperson for those who are not able to speak for themselves – advocating. • Being a friendly visitor or companion. • Working on a committee for a cause you care about. • Volunteering for a church, hospital, continuing care facility, school, sport, or other community program. • Volunteering for a community agency, such as a food bank, Habitat for Humanity, etc. • Volunteering at a fair or special event. • Helping immigrants settle in a new country. • Volunteering in less developed countries/ communities. • Hosting international students. • Contributing to positive family relationships. • Healing people through traditional or alternative medicine, massage, reflexology, or other therapies. • Teaching literacy skills. • Teaching English as a second language.

Interests/Skills Categories	Sample Activities for Work, Volunteer, or Leisure
Being Physically Active	• Walking, hiking, running, orienteering, geocaching. • Walking a dog. • Individual sports, such as skiing, cycling, skating, and swimming. • Competitive sports, such as golfing, squash, track and field, badminton, tennis, table tennis, and golf Frisbee. • Team sports, such as curling, hockey, volleyball, shuffleboard, bowling, soccer, ultimate Frisbee, badminton, pickle ball, and computer sports. • Adventure sports, such as rock climbing, rafting, sky diving, caving, and racing. • Nature activities, such as bird-watching, identifying plants, fishing, hunting, geocaching, orienteering, boating, sailing, metal detecting, gold panning, sightseeing, horse-back riding, and riding a quad or snowmobile. • Farming or forestry. • Tending, breeding, or training animals. • Gardening. • Landscaping. • Building or renovating your home, furniture, or other items. • Fixing things – troubleshooting. • Restoring automobiles. • Building models. • Playing games, such as pool, table tennis, or darts. • Meditative exercise such as, yoga, Tai Chi, qigong • Martial arts. • Dancing, such as country, tap, square, ballroom, salsa, line, or folk dancing • Personal fitness training. • Gym circuit training. • Computer fitness. • Going on a day trip. • Camping or trailering. • Traveling/exploring new areas. • Delivering flyers, newspapers, political literature, advertising, or promotional materials. • Being a secret shopper. • Being a flag person on a construction crew.

Interests/Skills Categories	Sample Activities for Work, Volunteer, or Leisure
Being Creative	• Drawing. • Painting. • Sculpting or pottery. • Drafting. • Creative writing. • Writing or formatting newsletters, reports, blogs, websites, and books. • Singing or playing a musical instrument for pleasure. • Performing for others. • Composing music. • Creating recipes, menus, or table decorations. • Cake decorating. • Home decorating. • Flower arranging • Dried flower creations. • Designing, architectural or technical designs. • Designing landscapes and gardens. • Designing crafts using fabric, wood, glass, gemstones, metal, or other materials. • Designing layouts. • Developing new ideas and innovations to create a product, service, or program. • Developing models or theories. • Publishing ideas. • Multimedia designing. • Photographing or videotaping. • Creating memory books/ scrapbooks, notepaper, card making. • Calligraphy, print designing. • Acting, interpreting, interpretive dancing. • Storytelling. • Inventing.

Interests/Skills Categories	Sample Activities for Work, Volunteer, or Leisure
Organizing People, Things, or Information	• Arranging for speakers and logistics • Catering functions. • Planning and coordinating a special event, such as a family gathering, fundraising, or community event. • Coordinating volunteers. • Conducting market surveys. • Making plans for future activities. • Making arrangements for planned activities • Organizing personal papers. • Keeping records for an organization. • Editing information. • Recording family genealogy and history. • Collecting things, such as antiques, dolls, cards, music, books, coins, or artifacts. • Classifying materials and information. • Organizing materials for storage or display. • Organizing space, such as rooms, closets, cupboards, garages, offices, or warehouses. • Organizing ideas and experience through journaling. • Coordinating stage, production, sports, or other events.
Using my Hands	• Cooking and baking. • Sewing and alterations. • Repairing tools, equipment, vehicles, appliances, or computers. • Restoring antiques or artifacts. • Wine or beer making. • Woodworking, metalworking, pottery, stained glass, or other skilled crafts. • Furniture refinishing. • Building models. • Doing handcrafts, such as knitting, weaving, quilting, embroidery, crocheting, needlepoint, beading, or jewellery. • Making gift baskets or seasonal giftware. • Driving/ operating a vehicle, equipment, or machinery. • Giving a massage or other therapeutic treatments.

Interests/Skills Categories	Sample Activities for Work, Volunteer, or Leisure
Leading or Influencing People	• Initiating a project, service, activity, event, or group. • Managing a project, event, group, or organization. • Acting as a liaison between two or more groups. • Leading or facilitating a group. • Developing or leading a training session. • Making a presentation. • Public speaking. • Writing informational materials for publication. • Negotiating contracts or resolutions. • Supervising a person or group. • Volunteering on a board of directors or committee. • Recruiting volunteers. • Fundraising. • Coaching sports participants. • Campaigning for a political party. • Promoting a cause. • Marketing or promoting a product, service, or event. • Selling a product or service. • Consulting for local, national, or international programs or projects. • Producing, directing, or managing performing arts.

Interests/Skills Categories	Sample Activities for Work, Volunteer, or Leisure
Interacting with People or Ideas	• Visiting with family or friends – at home or in a public place, such as a coffee shop. • Hosting a gathering in your home or in a public place. • Participating in a group with shared interests, such as a choir, book club, hiking group, church group, photography club, service club, or support group. • Being a sales associate. • Going to the library, book stores. • Researching information on the Internet. • Talking on the telephone, social networking sites. • Attending a religious service. • Attending a movie, cultural, or sports event. • Attending a fair, museum or exhibition. • Attending a meeting or information session. • Attending a social function, such as a lunch, dinner, or party. • Playing bingo or games of chance at a hall or casino. • Writing or responding to letters, memos, reports, blogs, tweets, email messages, or meeting notes. • Linking with others through online tools. • Watching television, listening to the radio. • Reading newspapers, magazines, or books, in print or online • Conducting a survey. • Participating in market research. • Providing information to the public. • Dining out in a restaurant.

Interests/Skills Categories	Sample Activities for Work, Volunteer, or Leisure
Using my Mind (Studying, Thinking, or Reasoning)	• Playing cards, chess, or other board games. • Playing computer or video games. • Solving puzzles, such as Sudoku, crossword, jigsaw, anagrams, or luminosity challenges. • Solving problems for others. • Reviewing and integrating ideas and information. • Developing objectives, strategies, and performance measures. • Developing or testing theories. • Interpreting statistics. • Studying or researching any subject of interest, on your own or by taking a class. • Researching vacation destinations. • Learning or using information technologies. • Learning to speak another language. • Learning about other cultures or geographic areas. • Developing computer programs. • Developing a website or mobile app. • Evaluating computer programs and systems. • Writing or negotiating proposals, business plans, or contracts. • Assessing organizational efficiencies. • Planning projects. • Keeping informed on current issues, events, information, or trends through reading, discussions, and online resources.
Managing Numbers and Money	• Being a treasurer or accountant for an organization. • Shopping for the best prices. • Estimating the cost of projects and plans. • Gathering statistics. • Investing in the stock market. • Keeping financial records. • Preparing a budget. • Paying bills. • Staying current with economic trends. • Taking inventory. • Preparing tax returns. • Analyzing cash flow. • Providing financial advice, credit counselling. • Teaching financial literacy.

Interests/Skills Categories	Sample Activities for Work, Volunteer, or Leisure
Household Chores and Personal Care	<ul><li>Daily living activities:<ul><li>— Meal planning and preparation.</li><li>— Cooking.</li><li>— Barbecuing.</li><li>— Baking.</li><li>— Washing dishes.</li><li>— Lawn and yard maintenance.</li><li>— Flower or vegetable gardening.</li><li>— Snow shovelling.</li></ul></li><li>Building maintenance and repair.</li><li>Vehicle maintenance and repair.</li><li>Appliance maintenance and repair.</li><li>Housecleaning.</li><li>Laundry and ironing.</li><li>Sewing.</li><li>Shopping...<ul><li>— for groceries.</li><li>— for your personal needs.</li><li>— for household items.</li><li>— for gifts.</li></ul></li><li>Managing waste – garbage, recycling, or composting.</li><li>Paying bills and banking.</li><li>Preparing income tax.</li><li>Personal grooming.</li><li>Arranging for and attending appointments, such as dentist, hairstylist, therapist, medical, financial, or legal advisor.</li><li>Driving others to appointments.</li><li>Family care-giving – caring for elderly family members, children, grandchildren, or dependent adults.</li><li>Caring for your pet.</li></ul>

Interests/Skills Categories	Sample Activities for Work, Volunteer, or Leisure
What specific or other transferable skills do you have that you'd like to use?	
What other interests or activities have you thought of trying?	

"The key to retirement's enjoyment is involving yourself to the fullest in something you love doing and trying new things that make you stretch a bit."

Julie Winkler, quoted at age 76, wood carver, kayaker, spiritual quester, and would-be astronomer

Appendix D: Sample Activities for Your Personality Temperament

All four personality temperaments: explore sample activities from your blend of colours. In retirement, find balance by trying activities that are imaginative or spiritual, playful or fun, or allow you to learn a new skill or study an area of interest.

Organized Gold Sample Activities

Work and Volunteer Activities

- ⊚ Work part time or full time, contract, casual, or seasonal – in a new or former career where your skills can be a stabilizing influence (e.g., election worker, census taker).

- ⊚ Do record keeping, budgeting, accounting, or tax preparation for yourself and/ or others.

- ⊚ Continue in professional affiliations, providing continuity and stability to the group or maintaining historical records.

- ⊚ Volunteer for an organization, either on a board or committee, or provide a service (e.g., community service agencies).

- ⊚ Volunteer at a local library or museum.

- ⊚ Help to maintain law and order or help others feel secure through involvements with block watch, the police, or a fraud prevention program.

- ⊚ Help others to read and write through a school or community literacy program.

- ⊚ Help newcomers settle by providing information on resources in the community.

Individual and Group Activities

- ◉ Join one or more groups that share common interests (e.g., a service club, faith community, band, choir, book club).

- ◉ Collect and organize information on your family history and/ or other areas of interest.

- ◉ Hobbies

- ◉ Stay current and discuss current event with others.

- ◉ Contact a local arts group and learn a new craft (e.g., painting, woodworking, spinning).

- ◉ Sports

- ◉ Join a fitness group (e.g., hiking group, Tai Chi, yoga, dancing, curling, or skiing group).

Inquiring Green Sample Activities

Work and Volunteer Activities

- ◉ Work part time, contract, casual or seasonal – in your field of expertise where you knowledge is valued and appreciated.

- ◉ Consult in an industry you know.

- ◉ Continue your professional affiliations, providing continuity, updating data and updated information, or writing manuals.

- ◉ Attend professionally affiliated conferences, or other functions in areas of interest.

- ◉ Volunteer on a board in the capacity of a strategist, analyzer, or problem solver (e.g., municipal, professional association, hospital boards, etc.).

⊚ Volunteer as a mentor or instructor.

⊚ Volunteer at a local museum.

Individual or Group Activities

⊚ Play bridge or other challenging games.

⊚ Work on a degree in a field of interest.

⊚ Take a course or study an area of interest.

⊚ Learn a new language.

⊚ Learn a new skill.

⊚ Write a book.

⊚ Invent something.

⊚ Hobbies

⊚ Research countries and cultures.

⊚ Read journals, books, articles.

⊚ Watch documentaries and current affairs programs.

⊚ Make your own wine or beer.

⊚ Design and maintain a website.

⊚ Sports

⊚ Involve yourself in individual sports (e.g, biking, walking, running, skiing) or team sports (eg. Masters sports events, golf, curling).

Resourceful Orange Sample Activities

Work and Volunteer Activities

- Promote events or sell products you enjoy.

- Perform at a comedy venue or improv theatre.

- Become a mystery shopper.

- Drive rented, sold, or leased vehicles to new locations.

- Drive a school, city, or handi-bus; drive others to appointments.

- Become a professional speaker, trainer, producer, writer, or photographer.

- Start your own business.

- Take your pet to visit seniors in retirement homes.

- Maintain lawns and gardens or do handy person jobs to allow seniors to stay in their own homes; maintain apartment, schools, or recreation facilities.

- Play or sing in a musical group.

- Build props or scenery for theatre.

Individual or Group Activities

- Throw surprise or spontaneous parties for friends and family members.

- Negotiate with others for the best deals.

- Adventure travel: hike, fish, ski, metal detect, or other outdoor pursuits.

- Build lawn furniture or ornaments.

ⓔ Renovate or decorate your own home.

Hobbies

ⓔ Try new foods and new restaurants.

ⓔ Write a blog to stay in touch with your family and friends.

ⓔ Do hands-on activities (e.g., woodworking, glass blowing, stained glass, crafts, cooking, gardening, wine making, picture framing, pottery, model railroading).

ⓔ Sports

ⓔ Compete in sports activities.

ⓔ Drive an ATV, quad, snowmobile, motorcycle, or race car.

Authentic Blue Sample Activities

Work and Volunteer Activities

ⓔ Become a motivational speaker.

ⓔ Volunteer at the pediatric or geriatric units at a hospital, a seniors' home, or community for those with disabilities.

ⓔ Help furnish a shelter in your community.

ⓔ Fundraise for refugees in a third world country.

ⓔ Mentor youth on a one-to-one basis or volunteer on a hotline.

ⓔ Support the arts by joining a board of directors or fundraising committee.

Individual and Group Activities

- Learn a new language.

- Have long leisurely lunches with special friends and/ or family members.

- Help family members (e.g., take care of a grandchild for a day).

- Attend the milestones of your family and friends whether small (e.g., kindergarten graduation, recitals, soccer games) or major (e.g., college or university graduation, decade birthdays, weddings).

- Visit family and friends who are unable to get out.

- Join a spiritual group or become more active in one in which you are already involved.

Hobbies

- Read books that bring you joy.

- Go for walks in natural areas to appreciate the scenery, plants, and animals.

- Photograph, paint, or draw the things you admire.

Sports

- Do yoga, Tai Chi, or some other non-competitive activity that will help enrich your well-being.

(Source: Retirement Dimensions™, Career/Life Skills Resources Inc.)

Remember these are only a few samples to spark ideas to start exploring.

Appendix E: Summer and Winter Calendars

"Everything is created twice – first you design it in your mind; then you do it."

Use these calendars to start planning a routine for your retirement life. Leave blank spaces for spontaneous activities or for rest.

It's easier to fill your calendar in the summer months. Winter poses a more difficult challenge for those who live at latitudes with both seasons. If that is your situation, it's important to design options for both seasons.

Spring/ Summer Calendar

	Monday	Tuesday	Wednesday	Thursday	Friday	Saturday	Sunday
Morning							
Afternoon							
Evening							

Fall/ Winter Calendar

	Monday	Tuesday	Wednesday	Thursday	Friday	Saturday	Sunday
Morning							
Afternoon							
Evening							

Appendix F: Solution to the Nine-Dot Puzzle

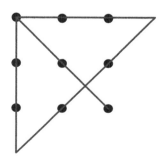

Appendix G: 10 Tips to Retire to the Life You Love

This is a quick guide to help you remember ideas from each chapter.

1. Phase your retirement. Instead of going abruptly from full-time work to full-time leisure, continue to work part time. Consult, do contract, temporary, or casual work. Start a new career, start your own business, or take on a project that interests you.

2. Know yourself, what is most important to you and what you love. Stay true to who *you* are, not someone else. Retire from the inside-out.

3. Join a group with like interests – the easiest way to stay socially connected. Social isolation is a common concern for retirees. Could a service club or book club be in your future?

4. Nurture the family relationships and friendships you want to keep; rekindle friendships that have lapsed; let go of friendships that are no longer in your best interest.

5. Continue to learn something – a new skill or new knowledge. Learning keeps you mentally alert, interested in the present and future, and interesting to others. Have you always wanted to play the guitar or learn another language? If not now, then when? Give it a try.

6. Keep physically active. Go for a daily walk – even without a dog. Cycle, swim, run, ski, try line dancing, or walk to a local coffee shop. Move more and sit less!

7. Volunteer for a cause you believe in, formally or informally, locally or globally. Contribute your talents, skills and wisdom for the greater good of your family, community, or society. Broaden your thinking from 'me' to 'we' and you will create new life meaning and purpose.

8. Adopt an attitude of gratefulness and compassion to yourself and others. Seek opportunities to express these daily to those whose paths you cross.

9. Be creative. Yes you can. We are all creative in our own way. Explore in what new ways you want to express your creativity: could it be art, music, inventing, quilting, scrap-booking, gardening, photography, writing, innovating, designing, crafting, woodworking, decorating? The possibilities are endless. Explore – give it a try. There's nothing to lose and who knows what you'll gain?

10. Last but not least, feed your soul. Meditate, pray, journal, read spiritual books, be in nature, do yoga, Tai Chi, listen to music... all great ways to de-stress and Just Be. Follow this advice found on a park bench:

> *"Take the time to sit and ponder; let your mind and spirit wander.*
> *Enjoy the view, embrace the day*
> *Remember to take the time to play."*

RESOURCES AND REFERENCES

INTRODUCTION – AGING AND RETIREMENT

www.aarp.org – The American Association of Retired Persons

www.everythingzoomer.com – The Canadian Association of Retired Persons

www.nextavenue.org – Public Broadcasting Service publishes Next Avenue e-newsletter

www.fcac-acfc.gc.ca – The Financial Consumer Agency of Canada

www.taosinstitute.net/positive-aging-newsletter – by Kenneth and Mary Gergen

www.sage-ing.org – Sage-ing International

www.2young2retire.com – Reinventing retirement for baby boomers

Ken Dychtwald, Ph.D and Joe Flower, *Age Wave, The Challenges and Opportunities of an Aging America*, Jeremy P. Tarcher, Inc., 1989 www.agewave.com

Ken Dychtwald Ph.D., *Age Power*, Penquin Putnam Inc, 1999

Ken Dychtwald, Ph.D., *A New Purpose: Redefining Money, Family, Work, Retirement, and Success*, William Morrow Paperbacks, 2010

Lyndsay Green, *You Could Live a Long Time: Are You Ready?*, Thomas Allen Publishers, 2010

Zalman Schachter-Shalomi & Ronald S. Miller, *From Age-ing to Sage-ing: A Profound New Vision of Growing Older*, Warner Books, 1995

Rein Selles, Jim Yih, & Patricia French, *Ten Things I Wish Someone Had Told Me About Retirement*, 2013, www.retirementchallenge.com

Ernie Zelinsky, *How to Retire Happy, Wild, and Free: Retirement Wisdom That You Won't Get from Your Financial Advisor*, Ten Speed Press, 2004

PART I – SIX WAYS TO LOVE YOUR LIFE

Chapter 1 – The Six Circles of Life

Chapter 2 – Be Who You Are

www.career-lifeskills.com – Career/ LifeSkillls Resources Inc. – publishes Retirement Dimensions

www.personalitydimensions.ca

Linda Berens, *Understanding Yourself and Others, An Introduction to the 4 Temperaments 4.0*, Radiance House, 2010

Susan Cain, Quiet, *The Power of Introverts in a World That Can't Stop Talking*, Crown Publishers, 2012

Isabel Briggs Myers with Peter B. Myers, *Gifts Differing*, Consulting Psychologists Press, 1992

David Keirsey, *Please Understand Me II*, Prometheus Nemesis Book Company, 1998

Chapter 3 – Just Be

www.creativeaging.org – with local chapters in the USA and Canada

Mitch Albom, *Tuesdays with Morrie, An Old Man, A Young Man, and Life's Greatest Lessons*, Broadway Books, 1997

Brené Brown, *The Gifts of Imperfection: Let Go of Who You Think You're Supposed to Be and Embrace Who You Are*, Hazelden, 2010

Deepak Chopra & Rudolph E. Tanzi, Super Brain: *Unleashing the Explosive Power of Your Mind to Maximize Health, Happiness, and Spiritual Well-Being*, Harmony Books, 2012

Gene D. Cohen, *The Mature Mind: The Positive Power of the Aging Brain*, 2005

David K. Foote with Daniel Stoffman, Boom, Bust and Echo, Macfarlane, Walter, and Ross, 1996

Carl Honore, *In Praise of Slow: How a Worldwide Movement is Challenging the Cult of Speed*, Vintage Canada 2004

Bhante Gunaratana, *Mindfulness in Plain English*, Wisdom Publications, 2011

Jean Houston, *The Wizard of Us*, Atria Books, 2012

Phil Minnaar, Ph.D., *The Positive Dictionary, Only Words with Positive Messages*, Eksal Quality Systems, 2007

Osho, *Creativity: Unleashing the Forces Within*, Osho International Foundation, 1999

Osho, *Meditation for Busy People: Stress Beating Strategies to Calm Your Life*, Osho International Foundation, 2004

Gene Perret, *Unleashing Your Creativity After 50!* Quill Driver Books, 2008

Zalman Schachter-Shalomi & Ronald S. Miller, *From Age-ing to Sage-ing: A Profound New Vison of Growing Older*, Grand Central Publishing, 1995

Jill Bolte Taylor, *My Stroke of Insight: A Brain Scientist's Personal Journey*, Viking Press, 2006

Eckhart Tolle, *A New Earth: Awakening to Your Life's Purpose*, Penguin Group, 2005

Chapter 4 – Be Well

<u>www.cspinet.org</u>

The Centre for Science in the Public Interest – unsponsored research – publishes the *Nutrition Action Newsletter*

<u>www.livingto100.com</u> – The Life Expectancy Calendar

Neil Barnard M.D., *Power Foods for the Brain: An Effective 3-Step Plan to Protect Your Mind and Strengthen Your Memory*, Grand Central Life & Style, 2013

Walter M. Bortz II, *The Roadmap to 100, the Breakthrough Science of Living a Long, Healthy Life*, 2004

Walter M. Bortz II, *Diabetes Danger – What 200 Million Americans Need to Know*, 2005

Dan Buettner, *The Blue Zones, 9 Lessons for Living Longer – from the people who've lived the longest*, The National Geographic Society, 2012

Norman Doidge, *The Brain That Changes Itself – Stories of Personal Triumph from the Frontiers of Brain Science*, Penguin Group, 2007

Marla Heller, *The Dash Diet Action Plan – proven to lower blood pressure and cholesterol without medication*, 2007

Tedd Mitchell, Tim Church, & Martin Zuckers, *Move Yourself: The Cooper Clinic Medical Director's Guide to All the Healing Benefits of Exercise (Even a Little!)*, John Wiley & Sons, 2010

Reader's Digest, *Long Life Prescription, 2008* – based on 5000 clinical studies

Stephanie A. Silberman Ph.D., *The Insomnia Workbook – A Comprehensive Guide to Getting the Sleep You Need*, New Harbinger Publications, Inc, 2008

Chapter 5 – Be Compassionate

Janet Bray Attwood and Chris Attwood, *The Passion Test*, Hudson Street Press, Penguin Group, 2007 www.passiontestonline.com

Brene Brown, *The Gifts of Imperfection – Let Go of Who You Think You're Supposed to Be and Embrace Who You Are – Your Guide to a Wholehearted Life*, Hazelden, 2010

Gary Chapman, *The Five Love Languages, Singles Edition*, Moody Publishing, 2014 www.5lovelanguages.com

Gary Chapman, *The Five Love Languages: How to Express Heartfelt Commitment to Your Mate*, Northfield Publishing, 2004

Eric Klinenberg, Going Solo, *The Extraordinary Rise and Surprising Appeal of Living Alone*, Penguin Press 2012

Dalai Lama, *How to be Compassionate, a Handbook for Creating Inner Peace and a Happier World*, Atria Books, 2011

Abraham H. Maslow, *A Theory of Human Motivation*, 1943, originally published in Psychological Review, 50, 370-396

Roberta K. Taylor & Dorian Mintzer, *The Couple's Retirement Puzzle*, Sourcebooks, 2014

Chapter 6 – Be a Contributor

www.awebusiness.com – Alberta Women Entrepreneurs

www.canadabusiness.ab.ca – explore and start a business

www.cbsc.org – Canadian Business Service Centres

www.ceci.ca – Canadian Centre for International Studies and Cooperation www.charityvillage.ca – work opportunities in the not-for-profit sector

www.cciorg.ca – Canadian Crossroads International places older adults in positions involving education, sustainable resource and rural development

www.getvolunteering.ca – matches volunteers with organizations in Canada

www.globalvolunteers.org

www.metowe.com – Craig and Marc Kielburger – make a difference in your community

www.projects-abroad.net – a diverse range of international service opportunities

www.tesol.org – teachers of English to speakers of other languages

www.thirdage.ca – work opportunities for those 50+

www.voluntourism.org – global travel/ volunteer opportunities

www.workaway.info – travel, language, and work exchanges

www.wwoof.org – world-wide opportunities on organic farms

www.retiredworker.ca – where employers and employees find each other

Linda Berens, *Understanding Yourself and Others, An Introduction to the 4 Temperaments 4.0*, Radiance House, 2010

Richard N. Bolles and John E. Nelson, *2nd Edition What Color is Your Parachute for Retirement: Planning Now for the Life You Want*, 2010

Rhonda Byrne, *The Secret*, Atria Publishing, 2006

Donna Dunning, *What's Your Type of Career? Unlock the Secrets of Your Personality to Find Your Perfect Career* Path, Davies-Black Publishing, 2001

Government of Alberta, *Midlife Career Moves*, www.alis.alberta.ca publications, 2003

Barbara Jaworski, *Rebel Retirement – A KAA-Boomer's Guide to Creating and Living an Explosive Second Act*, Workplace Institute, 2011

Carolyn Kalil, *Follow Your True Colors to the Work You Love*, True Colors, Inc.,2002

Jo Parfitt & Colleen Reichrath-Smith, *A Career in Your Suitcase, 4th Edition*, Summertime Publishing, 2013

Mary Ann Peters, *The 50's Plus: to Work or Not to Work, an Opportunity to Examine Your Future Work Options*, iUniverse, 2007

Zalman Schachter-Shalomi & Ronald S. Miller, *From Age-ing to Sage-ing: A Profound New Vison of Growing Older, Grand Central Publishing*, 1995

Barbara Sher, *It's Only Too Late If You Don't Start Now; How to Create Your Second Life After 40*, Delacorte Press, 1998

Sun Life Financial, *Unretirement®* Index Report, 2014

David Whyte, *Crossing the Unknown Sea – Work as a Pilgrimage of Identity*, Riverhead Books, 2002

Chapter 7 – Be Curious

www.calgarylifelonglearners.ca – adults learning for the fun of it – start a chapter in your own community?

www.conted.ucalgary.ca – daytime and travel/study courses

www.coursera.org – free global online university courses

www.luminosity.com – online brain exercises

www.roadscholar.org – educational tours in 90 countries

www.routestolearning.ca –The Canadian Elderhostel organization

www.ted.com – informative talks by experts on a subject

Jill Bolte Taylor, *My Stroke of Insight: A Brain Scientist's Personal Journey*, Viking Press, 2006

Mihaly Csikszentmihalyi, *Finding Flow: The Psychology of Engagement with Everyday Life* Basic Books, Perseus Books Group, 1997

Gene D. Cohen, *The Mature Mind: The Positive Power of the Aging Brain*, 2005

Norman Doidge, M.D, *The Brain That Changes Itself: Stories of Personal Triumph from the Frontiers of Brain Science*, 2007

Wayne Dyer, numerous self-help books to be discovered online and in bookstores

Sondra Kornblatt, *A Better Brain at Any Age: the Holistic Way to Improve Your Memory, Reduce Stress, and Sharpen Your Wits*, Conari Press, 2009

PART II – DESIGN YOUR MEANINGFUL FUTURE

Chapter 8 – Define a Direction

Angeles Arien, *The Second Half of Life: Opening the Eight Gates of Wisdom*, Sounds True Inc., 2007

Tony Buzan with Barry Buzan, *The Mind Map Book*, A Plume Book, 1993

John D. Krumbolz and Al S. Levin, *Luck is No Accident – Making the Most of Happenstance in Your Life and Career*, Impact Publishers, 2007

Joyce Schwartz, *The Vision Board: The Secret to an Extraordinary Life*, Collins Design, 2008.

PART III – WHAT'S NEXT?

Chapter 10 – Understand the Transition to Retirement

William Bridges, *Managing Transitions, Making the Most of Change*, Da Capo Press, 2003

Government of Alberta, *Change and Transitions, The path from A to B is not always a straight line*, www.alis.alberta.ca/publications, 2002

Susan Jeffers, Ph.D., *Feel the Fear and Do it Anyway, dynamic techniques for turning fear, indecision, and anger into power, action, and love*, Ballantine Books, 2007

Spencer Johnson, *Who Moved My Cheese?* G.P. Putnam's Sons, 1998

Byron Katie, *Loving What Is: Four Questions That Can Change Your Life*, Three Rivers Press, 2003

Chapter 11 – Final Thoughts

Mike Dooley, *Choose Them Wisely: Thoughts Become Things*, Atria Publishing, 2009 www.tut.com/tutshop/

ABOUT THE AUTHOR

Nell Smith is the Creator and Founder of Retire to the Life You Design© workshops and presentations.

As a professional retirement planner and certified career development professional, she has inspired thousands of adults to plan their careers, find work, and prepare for a fulfilling retirement life.

Now in her 70s, Nell embodies the Six Circles of Life framework while living in Calgary, Canada with her husband.

Professional speakers and experienced facilitators who are trained associates of Retire to the Life You Design© are available to:

ⓔ Present at conferences, seminars, and 'Lunch and Learn' sessions

ⓔ Facilitate experiential workshops from half-day to full days

ⓔ Coach individual clients

ⓔ Customize our services to meet your needs

Our associates live across Canada and are available to travel to any location in the world.

We would love to help you help your members, employees, attendees, or clients retire to the life they love and design their own meaningful futures!

Please contact Nell:
nell@retiretothelifeyoulove.com
www.retiretothelifeyoulove.com
www.retiretothelifeyoudesign.com

ALSO AVAILABLE FROM
SUMMERTIME PUBLISHING

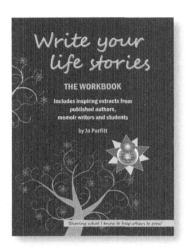

Lightning Source UK Ltd.
Milton Keynes UK
UKOW07f2012031214

242592UK00003B/79/P